D1572960

The Cinema of Federico Fellini

By the same author
The Hollywood Professionals
Vol. 4 (Tod Browning)

The Cinema of
Federico Fellini

Stuart Rosenthal

South Brunswick and New York: A.S. Barnes and Company
London: The Tantivy Press

A.S. Barnes & Co., Inc.
Cranbury, New Jersey 08512

The Tantivy Press
108 New Bond Street
London W1Y OQX

Library of Congress Cataloging in Publication Data

Rosenthal, Stuart.
   The cinema of Federico Fellini.

   Filmography: p.
   Bibliography: p.
   1. Fellini, Federico.   I. Title.
PN1998.A3F355 1975   791.43'0233'0924
ISBN 0-498-01450-9   73-13193

Jacket design by Stefan Dreja

SBN 0-904208-90-7 (U.K.)

PRINTED IN THE UNITED STATES OF AMERICA

Contents

Preface

In previously published books on Fellini, some authors view his work through the filter of their personal and professional relationships with the director while others restrict themselves to one or two significant aspects of his films—symbolism, for example, or spiritualism, or conflict with the church. Still others consider his films one by one or in groups, treating the Masina films, say, separately from *The White Sheik* and *Variety Lights*.

All of these methods can be illuminating, but each has its inherent pitfalls. Fellini's friends are likely to let their feelings for him interfere with their objectivity. Those who write about a few central themes necessarily ignore other important areas of Fellini's artistry. The film-by-film technique makes it easy to overlook vital relationships between films or groups of films. The blind spot left by these standard approaches has become all too obvious in the last few years when observers have expressed astonishment that *Roma* came from the man who once created *La strada*.

Here I have tried to achieve an overview of Fellini's work in order to get a sense of the direction his career has taken. I regard this study not as an exhaustive analysis of Fellini's films, but rather as a guide to a broad range of critical concerns in them. The book falls into three sections. Chapter One examines the link between Fellini and his characters *and* between the characters and the audience, stressing the shift from objectivity to personalism that has gradually taken place in his movies since the Forties. Once the close ties among Fellini, his characters, and his viewers are understood, it is possible to appreciate the formal side of Fellini's work as something more than just bravura effects. Chapters Two and Three are concerned with how Fellini's unique style of expression reflects his intense personal interest in his characters. The remainder of the book provides more extensive discussions of individual films. It emphasises their continuity with one another and traces a logical pattern of growth in the way Fellini has used increasingly innovative formats to deal with his own problems and obsessions. Accordingly, Chapter Four covers the films that focus upon Fellini through their characters, and Chapter Five those that present Fellini's perceptions directly, without the use of such intermediaries. This structure should help dissuade the critics who insist that Fellini underwent some sort of radical change between *La dolce vita* and *8½*.

One last note: some of Fellini's major themes will strike many readers as overworked when set out in print. The problem of communication, for example, was the object of widespread, though rarely penetrating discussion in the late Fifties. Since that time it has degenerated into something worse than a *cliché*. Yet, Fellini was making films about ineffective communication long before it became a fashionable topic at cocktail parties, and has continued to make them even though the subject is now considered trite. Moreover, he attacks the issue at such a basic human level that charges of pretension or lack of sophistication seldom arise. This, I feel, is a tribute to Fellini's honesty which, though conspicuously lacking in the interviews he gives, is a constant in his films.

Acknowledgements

This book would not have been possible in its present form without the help of a great many people. Myron Bresnick and Dorothy Desmond of Macmillan Audio Brandon Films and Don Krim of United Artists tolerated and obliged my repeated requests for screenings. Frank Pedi and Doug Lemza of Films, Inc., Bill Blair of United Films, and Alan Twyman of Twyman Films were equally helpful in arranging screenings. Edward Arthur of Arthur Theatres, St. Louis, provided 35mm projection facilities when they were needed. Kirk Karhi of New Line Cinema also loaned me prints.

For stills and related material, I am indebted to Dan Talbot (New Yorker Films), Robert Edelstein (Macmillan Audio Brandon), Don Krim (United Artists), Julian Senior (Warner Brothers), Peter Cowie, Nell Watts (Films, Inc.), Jim Loutzenheizer, Mario Longardi, RAI-TV, Unitalia, and New World Pictures.

I would like to thank George Fasel for his meticulous reading and commentary on the manuscript, Ken Plax for his editorial help and Barry Komm for typing the manuscript.

I would also like to thank Federico Fellini and Mario Longardi for their help and Lois and Francesco Mauro for their suggestions, explanations and hospitality in Rome.

I owe a special debt of gratitude to Mr. George McCue of the "St. Louis Post-Dispatch." Without his encouragement, both direct and indirect, I would not have had the opportunity to write this book.

N.B. extracts from the author's own interview with Fellini are indicated in the text thus**.

Superior numbers in the text refer to the annotated Bibliography at the back of the book.

The Cinema of Federico Fellini

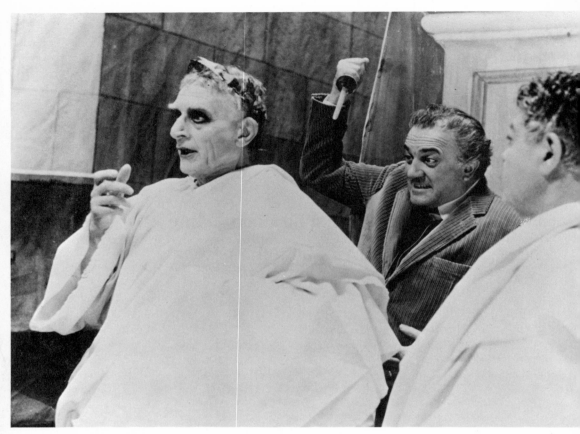

Fellini the actor: it is said that Fellini takes great pleasure in acting out the roles in his films himself. Here he stabs Caesar during the shooting of ROMA.

1
The Personal Vision

There are many possible ways for a viewer to interact with the content of a fiction film. He may view it objectively, judging the characters and their world on purely rational grounds. Such an approach enables him to apply his own values and intelligence to understanding the film, and to know where a character stands with respect to the environment or to other characters. The Italian neo-realists, for example, emphasised objectivity in dealing with the postwar social and economic climates. Their films took on added power because they seldom appeared manipulative. The spectator can also see things subjectively, from the point of view of a character in the film. In this case, he will appreciate, and usually look sympathetically upon, the character's feelings and behaviour. A third possibility is that the film may lead the viewer to accept the interpretation of its creator—usually the writer or director. Such personalism is particularly strong when the film-maker's inspiration comes from his life and obsessions, as in the work of Ingmar Bergman. Although a given film may elicit one or another of these effects predominantly, they are by no means mutually exclusive.

In watching a film by Federico Fellini, these different kinds of response work in concert, complementing, clarifying and expanding one another. Fellini models certain of his characters after himself, making his problems their problems. These autobiographical currents give the films, *a priori*, a degree of solicitude for the characters. Fellini amplifies this bias through techniques which make us see and feel as the character does. But the director realises that he and his creations do not always do, or even know, what is best for themselves. At times, therefore, he lets us see them from a distance, so we can recognise the sources and consequences of their mistakes. For Fellini, such objectivity can amount to a sort of self-criticism. The relative weights of objectivity, subjectivity and personalism in Fellini's work varies from film to film.

Fellini's first serious participation in film-making was with the neo-realists, the creators of one of the most objective movements in cinema history. He met Roberto Rossellini through his friend Aldo Fabrizi, the actor who plays the priest in *Open City* (1945). Prior to meeting Rossellini, Fellini's movie work had been limited to writing gags for rather slight comedies. As a script-writer, Fellini probably contributed little to *Open City*, but he learned a great deal about making a realistic film under almost impossible conditions. Fellini played a larger role in the genesis of *Paisa* (1946), acting as Rossellini's assistant and providing the idea for the monastery episode. His travels throughout Italy during the making of *Paisa* filled Fellini with enthusiasm for both the people he met and for the film medium. Even then, however, he may have been looking at reality differently than his collaborators. "Reality," he said, referring to the neo-realist era, "assailed us in such an amazing, exciting way that the real world we were photographing was in itself a feat of the imagination."[4]

The objective character of Fellini's work has changed and evolved since his association with the neo-realists. Though he later collaborated with Pietro Germi and Alberto Lattuada on films steeped in social ramifications, he points to Rossellini as having played the key role in the movement. "For me," Fellini said, "the only one to really make neo-realist films then was Rossellini. He was honest and open-minded and had cold eyes without tears. His films were not full of the sentimental. After the war, when the Fascist dictatorship was broken up, freedom was very precious. As a result, certain conditions existed and the situation had to be documented."** By the time Fellini started *Variety Lights* in 1950, the situation in Italy had changed considerably. Economic conditions improved at least to the point where it was reasonable to expand the boundaries which the neo-realists had, in conscience, imposed upon themselves. "Neo-realism means looking at reality with an honest eye," Fellini said of his work in the Fifties. "But any kind of reality; not just social reality but also spiritual reality, anything man has inside him."[41] Once it is conceded that the term neo-realism can have meaning when the goal is something other than the recording of prevailing social conditions, the problem of the so-called "neo-realist aesthetic" is reduced to a question of how a piece of material is presented. Fellini's films are certainly free of the artificiality that characterised the prewar Fascist cinema in Italy and that helped to instigate the neo-realist movement. Although heavily laden with subjective components, Fellini's work through *La dolce vita* (1959) retains much of neo-realism's direct style of observation. Thereafter, both his presentation of material and means of production have become increasingly removed from those of the neo-realists.

Fellini's explanation of neo-realism lays stress on documentation, open mindedness and lack of sentimentality. When the necessity for documentation had passed, he was free to work with dramatisations based upon his personal experience. Still, he maintained an important objectivity with regard to his subjects, even though they held special, frequently intimate, significance for him. Like the protagonists of *The White Sheik*, Fellini was raised in a small town and had many of his provincial ideas traumatically overturned on arrival in Rome. Therefore, a certain amount of sympathetic pathos might be expected in the character of Ivan Cavalli. He has great potential for turning into an endearing country clown and an audience

Fellini the actor: he shows Anita Ekberg how to greet the newsmen as she disembarks from the plane in LA DOLCE VITA.

normally commiserates with a man whose innocence is being trampled at each succeeding turn. Fellini, however, underlines the petty ambition and pride that increase Ivan's liability for what befalls him. As his encounters

Studio set: Fellini reconstructed part of Via Albalonga for the trattoria *sequence of ROMA.*

with the city and its people become progressively more absurd, the distance between him and the spectator increases. What might have been a warm, touching comedy transforms into an acid satire of both urban life and sham sophistication. Such treatment does not imply that Fellini is any less interested in Ivan Cavalli than he is in a more blatantly autobiographical character like Guido in *8½*. Fellini makes us feel Guido's sense of helplessness and frustration just as he has us share Ivan's confusion and desperation, but he never avoids showing Guido's egotistical, self-indulgent side. Though we experience Guido's feelings of harassment, the characterisation forces a detachment that prevents us from identifying with him. Almost everyone can understand the problems of Marcello in *La dolce vita* or Augusto in *Il bidone*, but it is inconceivable that many people will be able to see themselves in the place of the jet-set gossip journalist or the aging confidence man. This non-identification preserves the individuality of the character absolutely.

In his emphasis upon individuality, Fellini diverges from the neo-realist brand of objectivity, especially as practised by Vittorio De Sica and Cesare Zavattini. In *Bicycle Thieves* or *Umberto D*, the plight of one man is extended to represent that of perhaps a million other individuals. This is part of the broad documentary function of neo-realism. One can validly use devices to which the spectator has a predetermined, even sentimental response—the tears of a cute little boy or the loss of a dog, for example—

as long as they enhance the viewer's empathy with the characters. Such an approach helps convey the impact of the problem in terms that are readily comprehensible to people of every nationality and social stratum. Fellini, in contrast, is concerned with characters for their own sakes, rather than as symptoms of political or economic ills. André Bazin thought that Fellini was "the film-maker who has gone furthest in the neo-realist aesthetic; he has gone so far that he has crossed it and come out on the other side."[42] Instead of using personal tragedies to understand a social problem, Fellini is interested in the effect that society and its institutions have on his rather singular characters.

The initial sequence of *Nights of Cabiria* is almost a conscious acknowledgement of this distinction. First we see a young woman running across a field toward the river. She is frolicking with her lover who snatches her purse and shoves her into the water. Some nearby youths pull her from the river and several bystanders resuscitate her. The beginning of the action is all in long shot (except for a quick close-up of the boyfriend before he pushes her). The victim could be anybody and the camera might have witnessed this crime by chance. As the woman starts to sink, the emphasis shifts to the mechanics of the life-saving operation. Again, we do not see the woman's features; her face does not become visible until she begins, unexpectedly, to revile her rescuers. In this instant she acquires a personality and we know we have found the heroine of the film. It is as though Fellini

Historical recreation: Fellini offers his own version of the Fratellini Brothers performing for mental patients in I CLOWNS.

has focused down from a broad view of the hazards faced by prostitutes as a class (the neo-realist perspective) on to a single, unique case. Interestingly, critics often cite *I vitelloni* as Fellini's most neo-realistic film. It also happens to be the film in which the characters are the most familiar, the most universal.

While the neo-realist director tried to be as inconspicuous as possible, allowing the material to speak for itself, Fellini inserts his own interpretation between the audience and his subject matter. *I clowns* and *Roma* are literal instances of Fellini as moderator. The city explored in *Roma* does not exist apart from Fellini, and the historical impressions of the great clowns are entirely those of the director. "Un agenzia matrimoniale" is a more subtle example of the director's presence in an otherwise objective realm. This short film is the third sketch in Zavattini's *Love in the City* and Fellini's only directorial contribution to a work that is neo-realist by intent. Purporting to be journalistic efforts, the other segments of *Love in the City* emphasise the integrity of their investigative methods. Without commentary, Dino Risi sets up and records an evening in a dance hall. Alberto Lattuada affects a "candid camera" style to observe "fortuitous" street encounters between men and women. Francesco Maselli attempts a straight-forward re-creation of the trials of a young mother who abandoned her baby in Rome. Michelangelo Antonioni interviews unsuccessful suicides as they re-enact their attempts.

Fellini narrates his section through a reporter who is assigned to do a story about the clientele of marriage bureaux. But the reporter, ostensibly the director's representative, becomes a central character, and his reaction to the material supercedes the material itself. Several subjective shots are used as the reporter follows a parade of small children through the corridors leading to the agency's suite. The spritely musical accompaniment vanquishes the mood of desperation established by the preceding Antonioni study. From his vantage point, the narrator detects a certain quaintness in the idea of someone seeking a spouse through an agency. He is obviously as prepared to be amused as Antonioni was to find despair. His expectations are borne out when he finds an oily looking man, standing in a peculiar posture in the waiting room. The manager later explains that the man's parents are trying to find a wife for him, and that she must have long, blonde tresses as the primary requisite. This kind of eccentricity, so fascinating to Fellini, would be anathema to the strict neo-realist. The screen journalist, it emerges, has not done his homework and has no story to give the agency's consultant. He quickly fabricates a wealthy friend, a were-wolf, who desires a bride for therapeutic reasons. The jest yields more information about the company's business practices than could ever have been obtained with a more conventional request. Without a moment's hesitation the consultant opens her files. "Some girls have even vowed to marry a blind or disabled veteran," the manager explains, as he casually cuts a border around a sheet of paper. "We even found a wife for a mute."

Several days later the reporter is awakened by a phone call from the

Objectve vision: the disordered, threadbare apartment indicates the desperate qual- ity of Emma's life with Marcello in LA DOLCE VITA. Emma is played by Yvonne Furneaux.

agency. They have found a prospective wife for the werewolf. The reporter drives the candidate into the country for an interview and learns that she is the oldest of nine children of a poor, unemployed tenant farmer. She left home to get a job and, after three days without food, responded to the agency's newspaper advertisement. That is the episode's neo-realist core and link to the rest of the film: there are probably thousands of women in her predicament on the streets of Rome. But in observing the girl from the narrator's position, we find that she also has many engaging qualities of her own, especially her sincere goodheartedness. After listening to a description of the werewolf's horrible spells, she asks only, "Is he kind?" obviously having understood nothing. She declines the offer of a cigarette for herself, but asks if she may take it to give to her brother. She also dis- plays a meticulous cleanliness, refusing to sit on the grass for fear of soiling her dress and carefully brushing off her coat as she enters the automobile. The reporter has clearly been moved by these traits as much as by her story. He even goes so far as to advise her to forget all about the agency. Fellini has subverted the neo-realist intentions of *Love in the City* both by stressing a unique, individual case and by psychologically loading the re- cording mechanism from the personal side.

With time, the personalism in Fellini's work has grown to the point of all but squeezing out any objective understanding of his material. *8½* was the last of his films to maintain a significant degree of dispassion toward

Objective vision: above, Cabiria (Giulietta Masina) seems to clash with the elabo-rate decor of the actor's apartment—the conflict, in NIGHTS OF CABIRIA, tells us that her adventure there is bound to end unhappily; below, Iris (Giulietta Masina) and Picasso (Richard Basehart) are obviously out of their element at Rin-aldo's New Year party in IL BIDONE.

its subject. *Juliet of the Spirits* emphasises the central character's subjective responses, while the world of *Satyricon* springs entirely from the director's mind. *I clowns* and *Roma* are so personal as to be partially inaccessible to those who have not followed Fellini's preoccupations through his previous work. *Roma*, in fact, is selfishly conservative in its expression of fear at the changes being wrought by a new age and by a generation to which Fellini cannot relate. It is an escape into a private nostalgia and a plea for the retention of the comfortable values of the past. *Amarcord* is even more personal than *Roma* in its attempts to reconcile Fellini's past attitude toward his childhood with his current way of thinking.

As Fellini's art has become more and more personal there has been a corresponding decrease in the feeling of timelessness that attended his earlier films. Within its short running time, *I vitelloni* seems to capture the full human and territorial expanse of the coastal village in which it is set. The multiplicity and diversity of the protagonists, the variation in emotional tone from episode to episode, and the range of the landscape from beach to town to surrounding countryside promote the feeling of many things happening simultaneously. The incorrigibility of Fausto, Alberto, Leopoldo and Riccardo, coupled with Moraldo's restlessness, indicate that life in the town has been as we see it for many years and that it will go on in the same fashion indefinitely. This self-perpetuation is visually confirmed by the receding shots of Moraldo's friends and family as he departs on the train. This movement implies that Moraldo is moving forward in time while the others are staying where they are. The absence of temporal circumscription makes the events of the film seem less carefully selected, heightening its appearance of objectivity. By the same token, *Nights of Cabiria* begins and ends with Cabiria's betrayal by a man whom she thinks is in love with her. There is every reason to believe that the cycle will continue. And *La dolce vita* is simply a selection of episodes from a critical period of Marcello's life. He is in the middle of one when the film opens and at its conclusion we are as uncertain of his next step as he is. In *8½* and *Juliet of the Spirits*, on the other hand, we assume that the principal characters will keep growing and maturing after the film has ended. If so, everything we have witnessed will become a closed chapter of their lives. The memories of *Roma* and *Amarcord* are clearly isolated in time, and by reviving them on the screen, Fellini is putting them behind him once and for all.

The change in Fellini's attitude toward location work, another mode of operation carried over from his neo-realist experience, indicates how the subjective and personal visions have progressively displaced the objectivity in his films. *I vitelloni, Il bidone, Nights of Cabiria* and *La strada* are all more convincing for being shot in the places where the events they depict could actually have occurred. Daytime street scenes in particular benefit from the authenticity. But Fellini also uses locations for metaphorical and atmospheric purposes. especially piazzas at night, woods, open fields and beaches. They acquire a plane of meaning beyond their existence as mere sites where something can happen. This second level of meaning is all-important in *La dolce vita*, where the settings must convey the same lack of foundation as the characters' lives. Appropriately, Steiner lives in the bleached monotony of Mussolini's EUR section of Rome. In April, 1972, on the RAI-TV program "Io e . . .," Fellini selected this district as one of his favourite works of art. He explained that to him it resembled an enormous set at Cinecitta that will be torn down when the film it was built for is completed. EUR was available for *La dolce vita* and Fellini exploited it well, but he used it primarily for its appearance of artificiality. He might have been able to achieve essentially the same effect if Steiner's neighbourhood and apartment building had been constructed on a studio lot in collaboration with an architect. Only one scene in *8½* was shot on an unreconstructed location, while the fantastic worlds of *Juliet of the Spirits* and *Satyricon* precluded the use of natural settings.

Taking even a step beyond *Satyricon*, *Roma* completely inverts the neo-realist ethic of location filming. In Fellini's first four or five films, it is genererally not necessary to identify the square or street corner that appears in a shot. One piazza can stand for any of a hundred others. The viewer who is unable to place Broderick Crawford's meeting with his daughter as being near Piazza di Spagna has lost nothing, although recognition of the intersection may enhance the scene's verisimilitude for someone familiar with

Subjective vision: Gelsomina (Giulietta Masina) looks at the sleeping Zampano (Anthony Quinn) as a child might, prying open an eyelid to see if he is still there. From LA STRADA.

Subjective vision: Wanda's fanciful view of the The White Sheik (Alberto Sordi), suspended at an impossible height. In objective terms, this fantasy impresses us as absurd. From THE WHITE SHEIK.

Rome. (Specific places are more important, however, in *Nights of Cabiria* where Via Veneto and Ostia Road carry connotations of economic class.)

In *Roma*, Fellini reconstructs specific existing sites—a stretch of the Raccordo Anulare highway, a certain *trattoria*, the new subway excavation—on the Cinecitta lot, despite the fact that their real counterparts are only a short drive away. More is involved here than the impracticality of taking over the originals for a few weeks of movie-making. Fellini is dealing with his personal impressions, memories and imaginings rather than with the landmarks as they appear objectively. At the studio, he can exert complete control and can shut out ambiguity in order to heighten selectively whichever feature of the landscape is of concern to him. Under his supervision, an ordinary ribbon of pavement is transformed into an angry, tumultuous throughway and the descent into the Metro becomes a surrealistic journey. *Roma* is a striking demonstration of how far Fellini has removed himself from neo-realist objectivity. Location footage is used in *Roma* only when Fellini wants to make the city appear endangered. The counter-culture people appear to maraud the Spanish Steps and Piazza Ste. Maria in Trastevere, while the monuments shown at the end of the film seem to be at the mercy of the cyclists.

One does not capture the full impact of an event just by photographing it realistically. In *I clowns*, Fellini visits the Paris headquarters of ORTF to view a rare film featuring an appearance by Rhum, reputedly the greatest clown in history. The director and his crew have high expectations after having received many glowing descriptions of the legendary performer. But after the film clip has been run, they feel that it has let them down. It is not just the brevity of the strip that disappoints them, but its failure to tell them what it was like to witness a performance by the famed artist.

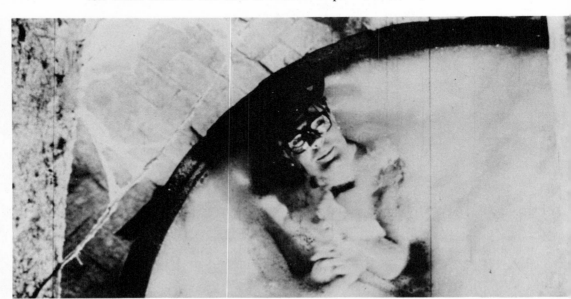

Subjective vision: Guido (Marcello Mastroianni) fantasises himself back to the farmhouse where, as a child, he enjoyed baths in a huge vat. From 8½.

The film, which shows Rhum going through one routine, is nothing more than a record of his features, dress and movements. It leaves the viewer without any first-hand knowledge of the excitement or pleasure generated by the act. Later, Fellini and Pierre Etaix try to watch an old movie of the three Fratellini brothers, but are stymied by a malfunctioning projector. Undeterred, Fellini offers several original re-creations of their performances. His fabrications capture the warmth and gentle funniness of the trio and are probably far superior to any documentary footage Etaix could have provided. Fellini insists that film make the spectator feel as though he were a participant in the events it reproduces.

Fellini is uncannily adept at making us feel reality as he or his characters feel it. His images incorporate not only the narrative side of the action, but also the emotional and physical sensations attendant on it. Toby Dammit (in the *Spirits of the Dead* sketch) fondles the shift lever and steering wheel of his Ferrari in the same way that he lovingly caresses his glass of whisky, bringing out the physical sensuality that the car and the drink have for him. In *I vitelloni*, the ferocious wind conveys the magnitude of Leopoldo's hopelessness when he discovers that Natali's interest in his play is merely the prelude to a sexual advance. Ivan Cavalli is literally pinned against a wall, wedged between the camera and the hard, stone exterior of a building, as he frantically grasps for an excuse for Wanda's absence to appease his relatives. As she returns from Bishma's, Giulietta's feelings of isolation and her smouldering desire to break free from them are expressed in the way her red and green clothing stands out in the greyness of the automobile's interior. The *Variety Lights* troupe are ebullient, if a trifle weary, as they set out for Renzo's country estate. The road they take seems to ramble and there are occasional stops for such diversions as listening to their host run through a chorus of "Figaro." When they return, however, the road seems very hard and linear in the morning light. The rows of trees that line it on either side appear in reverse perspective from the arrival shots, and the fatigued performers move slowly and painfully. A farmer with a lumbering pair of oxen passes the group. The scene imparts the physical and spiritual exhaustion brought on by the evening's aborted festivities.

This list of examples could be expanded to include virtually every scene in every Fellini film. In each case the character's point of view is intensified for the audience. We share Toby Dammit's soaring sense of power as he makes his Ferrari hurtle through the night and our understanding of Leopoldo's despair goes beyond a simple appreciation of the metaphor of the wind blowing every thing away. We feel as though we, too, have suffered through the cold and bitterness of his night on the beach with the actor. The same holds true for Cavalli's distress in a moment of pressing social claustrophobia, of the weariness of the music hall troupe and of Giulietta's loneliness in the midst of people. Experiencing things with the characters enables us to know them better than would ever be possible by simply observing their reactions. Cabiria's refusal to accept the clear evidence that

Personal vision: this prostitute from ROMA is apparently a version of La Saraghina, a sexual figure from Fellini's childhood.

Giorgio tried to drown her helps characterise her in terms of behaviour. But we cannot begin to understand or appreciate this behaviour until we have accompanied her through a series of disappointments and humiliations. Only by this means do we see beneath her false pride and sense her need to be recognised as part of something bigger than herself. Since, in the films from *I vitelloni* to *Juliet of the Spirits*, Fellini endeavours to familiarise us intimately with his characters, the process of reproducing their specific psychological and emotional realities is of vital importance.

At first it may seem contradictory to say that Fellini wants us to experience things just as his characters do, but not to identify with them. To know a character, however, it is necessary to view him from several angles. People have romantic notions about themselves and Fellini's characters are particularly skilful at transferring the blame for their problems to external factors. If we accepted Augusto's picture of himself, he would look

Personal visioin: the tobacconist in AMARCORD is another version of La Sara-ghina. Titta (Bruno Zanin), however finds her hard to handle.

like a brilliant swindler who got a lot of bad breaks. Marcello and Guido would come close to being martyrs, constantly dogged by people who irritate them and misunderstood by those whom they need. Marcello, for example, is often annoyed by Emma. She makes unreasonable demands at inopportune moments, like the telephone call during Sylvia's press conference. Worse still, Emma tries to confine her lover with *bourgeoise* ideals of love and domesticity. While we fully appreciate Marcello's consternation, we notice something he himself does not acknowledge—that he has misused Emma. The desolate existence he has provided for her in their dark, empty apartment is as much a dead end as the "living room-bedroom" life she offers him. But it is convenient for Marcello to have her available when he needs a companion or a respite from the hectic circles in which he moves. Sending her away would be too distasteful and require too great an effort, so Marcello, in his moral sloth, adopts a resigned attitude that only

Personal vision: Giudizio, the village idiot, appears in I VITELLONI, ROMA, I CLOWNS and AMARCORD. He is another figure from Fellini's boyhood in Rimini. Still from ROMA.

perpetuates her nagging.

While our position of objectivity compensates for a character's limited insight, our access to the character's sensorium and emotions helps us screen out our own prejudices. Our subjective rapport with Marcello prevents us from condemning him outright for his treatment of Emma. Knowledge of his insecurity and dissatisfaction makes us sympathetic to his selfish indecisiveness. In *I vitelloni*, we are moved by Fausto's panic and dejection when Sandra leaves him, although we realise objectively that he has provoked the desertion. For Fellini, human qualities and subjective needs are always more important than adherence to logical or perscribed forms of behaviour.

Besides giving us a true picture of a character, in contrast to his or her self-image, our ability to view the film objectively permits a realistic assessment of a given situation. Often, when we understand something that a character does not know, the sequence takes on an element of suspense which increases our concern for that character. The lavish house of the actor in *Nights of Cabiria* fascinates the gullible little prostitute and holds the promise of a change in fortune for her. Objectively, however, it is apparent that the ornamental luxury of the dwelling—with its vast rooms and mirrored panels—clashes violently with Cabiria's natural simplicity. We know that her adventure there must end in disappointment—and this knowledge intensifies the anxiety we feel for her. Similarly, we clearly discern that Rinaldo is indulging in a scornful practical joke by inviting the swindlers of *Il bidone* to his New Year's Eve celebration. The trio is obviously out of place at the party, but their behaviour indicates that they believe the invitation was extended in earnest. Augusto keeps trying to sell his uninterested host on a loan shark operation while Roberto, certain that he has "hit the big time," clumsily attempts to make new business connections. Picasso and Iris try naively to enjoy the high-powered brawl as though it were a family get-together. Because we know that the invitation was offered maliciously, the couple's discomfort comes through with much more force than if we were viewing the party strictly from their point of view. The same process makes Augusto look more pathetic and causes uneasiness over Roberto's recklessness.

Fantasy is a level of subjective character reality that is often at odds with the truth. In *The White Sheik*, Fellini makes fun of the secretary's statement that "our dreams are our real lives," and yet acknowledges that people tend to give more credence to what they would like to be true than they do to the hard facts of their existences. This early comedy is a model of how, in Fellini's films, a character's experiences, (or *way of experiencing*) are determined by the interaction of his aspirations and desires with external reality. The young bride is so immersed in the fanciful world of *The White Sheik* that seeing it in production with its bare bones exposed does not, in the least, shake her faith in the *fumetti*. She is still easily taken in by Fernando Rivoli's story about how his present wife poisoned his true love. When confronted by the wife after the disastrous seduction attempt, Wanda hurls accusations of sorcery at the woman, oblivious to her own position as a suspected adulteress. Rita Rivoli, the wife, is a hulking monster of a woman—a portrait that is played, for comic effect, against Sordi's femininity and Wanda's petiteness. But Rita's appearance is also in keeping with Wanda's belief that she is a witch. Thus Wanda's comprehension of the encounter is the product of her fairy tale life in collision with reality. The whole incident on the beach at Fregene fails to weaken her attachment to her romantic ideals and she begins her dictated suicide note by repeating the dramatic assertion, "Dreams are our real lives . . . but sometimes they plunge us into a fatal abyss."

A character's illusions about himself can constitute another level of fantasy. In *I vitelloni*, even an outside observer might take Giulia's playful throwing of *confetti* as a pass at Fausto, but her subsequent expression of embarrassment and regret corrects this impression. Fausto, however, in the sway of his Don Juan complex, is blind to the display of remorse and interprets her later rebuffs as additional enticements. When he explains to Sandra and Moraldo that Giulia got him fired because he resisted her advances, it is evident that he is not lying so much as rearranging the experience in his mind to make it compatible with his view of himself.

In *La strada*, the naivety of Gelsomina's expectations often throws the physical world into striking and unusual relief. This is particularly noticeable in the sequence with Oswaldo, in the stark terror of the attempted theft from the convent, and in the introduction to the religious festival with the almost magical entrance of the three musicians. But, most important of all, her lack of scepticism keeps us from dismissing Zampano as a mere brute, thereby humanising him and preventing him from looking like an outright villain. Gelsomina views her master through the eyes of a child, with an unassuming trust which will not allow her to condemn wholeheartedly the strongman's callousness. Because of her illusions, our acquaintance with Zampano is, in human terms, rewarding rather than revolting. Gelsomina is frequently called the most "Chaplinesque" of Fellini's creations and although this comparison stems mainly from Masina's superb mimickry, the closest parallel between Chaplin and Gelsomina is their involvement in a sort of childish fantasy world. "The peculiarity of Chaplin," Eisenstein wrote in his essay "Charlie the Kid," "consists of the fact that, despite his gray hairs, he has preserved a child's outlook and a spontaneous perception of events. Hence his freedom from the 'manacles of morals' and his ability to see in a comic spectacle that which causes others' flesh to creep. Such a trait in an adult is called 'infantilism.'"* Here is the crux of the Fellini-Chaplin affinity. Fellini's child's vision spares him from the demands of sophistication and the philosophical nuances of morality. He

*Leyda, Jay (editor), "Film Essays and a Lecture by Sergei Eisenstein," Praeger: New York, 1970, p. 110.

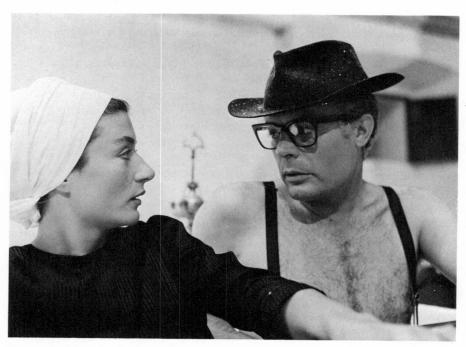

Personal vision: in the harem sequence of 8½, Guido wears the hat which marks him as an incarnation of Fellini. Marcello Mastroianni and Anouk Aimée.

is free to show unqualified affection for his characters in spite of their most serious shortcomings, and to monitor the world in terms of his own needs and those of his characters. Later in these pages we will examine the role played by "childhood mysticism" in the lives of Fellini's characters, but for now we need only note that patterns of feelings, beliefs and desires retained from childhood frequently determine the character's reaction to the obstacles of adulthood. The idealisations of childhood are a kind of living fantasy for the grown-up who holds on to them, particularly for Gelsomina, Giulietta in *Juliet of the Spirits*, Guido in *8½*, and Marcello in *La dolce vita*.

Of all Fellini's films, *8½* is most explicit in treating fantasy as a determinant of character reality. Guido is forever attempting to evade the pressures and frustrations of the moment by working them into the secure and ordered framework of boyhood. Thus, when he is troubled by feelings of isolation, he flashes back to the farmhouse where kindly old women once took care of him. Later, anticipating a confrontation between his wife and mistress, he daydreams himself back to the farmhouse, where he exercises complete mastery over not only Carla and Luisa, but every other woman who has figured in his life. Fantasy does not simply direct Guido's response to external reality—it *is* that response. At the film's conclusion, in a fantasy sequence, past and present are unified into a single reality.

When Fellini deals with semi-autobiographical protagonists, one expects that the character's experiences and attitudes will frequently coincide with that of the director. Indeed, the recovery and evaluation of childhood experience is central to Fellini's most recent films. *I clowns* and *Roma* start with vivid evocations of Fellini's schooldays and then examine the changes that have taken place in his world since that era. Furthermore, certain incidents and personalities from Fellini's own life repeatedly find their way, in different forms, into the lives of his characters. For example, the massive, earthy, sensual La Saraghina (a boyhood memory described in the books by Angelo Solmi[12] and Deena Boyer[3]) appears in various incarnations in Fellini's personal memoirs—as Anita Ekberg in *I clowns* and as the prostitutes in *Roma*. She carries similar connotations for Guido in *8½* and for Marcello when she appears in the person of Sylvia in *La dolce vita*. In a like manner, Volpina and the tobacconist embody the Saraghina mystique for Titta in *Amarcord*.

The term *personal cinema* immediately calls to mind the names Fellini and Bergman. Their films are, however, personal in very different ways. Bergman delves into questions and problems that are of special significance to him and applies his soulful thoughts and musings to a varied array of individuals and circumstances. Fellini, on the other hand, presents his obsessions in a less refined form. He emphasises immediacy—the gut-level panic and discontent brought on by such phobias as the fear of creative dessication, the coming of old age or the knowledge of isolation. Consideration of the complex philosophical ramifications of these dilemmas provides little or no comfort for Fellini, so he seldom has the inclination to penetrate beyond their first level of awareness. In this light, Fellini's films are seen to be essentially non-intellectual, and perhaps even anti-intellectual. Bergman's characters regularly analyse their position in lengthy dialogue passages. Fellini, for the most part, avoids such explicit verbal examinations. In "The Two Hundred Days of 8½," Deena Boyer describes how the exchange between Guido and Luisa after the screen test was modified from its original text, making it reactive rather than explanatory.

> Fellini has just written the dialogue. Then he changed several things. Originally, Guido's last line was: "Luisa, I need you—I swear I do." Hard with bitterness Luisa was to have answered "You don't need anyone. You've created emptiness around you." But at the last minute Guido's line becomes, "Don't be melodramatic." This evokes a different reaction from Luisa; a shudder as if she has been slapped. "It's a good thing you made me come here. It was time to reach a decision. And I assure you I won't back out of it. Go to Hell!"[3]

Daumier, the critic in *8½*, is the antagonist of Fellini's concept of personal cinema. He drones on, demanding objectivity and intellectuality, assuring Guido that nobody could possibly be interested in his childhood perceptions, and imploring him to tighten the film's structure and define its symbols. Predictably, Daumier is the most tiresome member of Guido's entourage. And if *8½* leaves any doubt as to Fellini's feelings toward those who insist that a film produce explicit statements, the topic is covered with finality in *I clowns*. A journalist, his pen eagerly poised, inquires of the

Personal vision: Trimulchio's banquet in SATYRICON is part of a world which exists only in the director's mind.

Personal vision: both Fellini and Ingmar Bergman have created cinemas which are highly personal, and both have depicted their obsessions as taunting demons. The demons in Bergman's HOUR OF THE WOLF (above) are those of the artist, while those in JULIET OF THE SPIRITS (below) are—as one might expect of Fellini—those of the past. The climaxes of these two films have the same mocking, threatening tone which hints at the compulsion the directors must feel in dealing with the themes the demons represent.

director, "And what message are you trying to give us in this film, Mr. Fellini?" Before Fellini can open his mouth to reply, a plastic bucket thrown by an offscreen clown lands on his head. A few seconds later, another hits the reporter.

When a Fellini character does make a philosophical statement, it usually sounds simplistic, or functions as a handy rationalisation. Il Matto's "everything has a purpose" speech in *La strada* is a good example. The speech works well as a device to satisfy temporarily Gelsomina's ongoing need of an identity. On the allegorical plane, noting Il Matto's role as "the wise fool" or a Christ figure, it is a representative expression of faith. Its impact as dogma is deliberately weakened by its interpreter's frivolous antics throughout the sequence. The speech, then, is an attempt to put life into some kind of order, rather than the exposton of a doctrine espoused by the director.

In terms of treatment, Bergman has many alternatives compared to Fellini. Thus Bergman's investigation of the nature and methods of the artist can be handled as well in a period film like *The Magician* as in *Shame* or *The Rite*, which are vague with respect to time and place; the artist can be embodied in such diverse figures as Albert Johansson in *Sawdust and Tinsel*, Elisabeth Vogler in *Persona* and Johan Borg in *Hour of the Wolf*. Each film is a rigorous, carefully constructed exploration of its themes within whatever framework Bergman deems most suitable to his intentions. Fellini, in contrast, draws upon events from his life as both material and format for most of his films. Certain *motifs* stemming from Fellini's own past experience recur regularly in his work. The young man coming to Rome from the provinces, as Fellini did in 1939, is found in *The White Sheik*, *I vitelloni*, *La dolce vita* and *Roma*. It is said that *I vitelloni* accurately depicts the atmosphere and life-style of his native Rimini, and that his father was very close to the character played by Annibale Ninchi in *8½* and *La dolce vita*.[12] Other recollections of Rimini manifested in Fellini's films include his Catholic schooldays, La Saraghina, Giudizio the village idiot, and the Oswaldo character in *La strada*.

Many of his films have characters that may be taken, to some extent, as representing the director himself. The most obvious of these is Guido in *8½*, who even wears the hat and cape which have become trademarks for Fellini. Peter Gonzales, as the young Fellini in *Roma*, wears these accessories, as does the man standing in for Mastorna in *Fellini: A Director's Notebook*. (*The Voyage of Mastorna* is one of Fellini's unrealised projects) The school uniform and cape single out Fellini as a child in *8½*, *Roma* and *La strada*. Most recently, in *I clowns* and *Roma*, Fellini has frankly identified the personifications of himself as a boy and even stood before the camera in person.

There are a few reasonably well established points about Fellini's life that may shed some light upon his material and his way of making films. His father was the travelling representative of a grocery company and, like Marcello's papa in *La dolce vita*, the elder Fellini's work kept him away from his family for extended periods of time. At the age of eighteen, Federico moved from Rimini to Rome, where he held a number of jobs, many of which demanded a creative sense of humour. At various times, he was on the staff of several comic and satiric publications, including the irreverent "Marc' Aurelio." He even produced a number of *fumetti* features—some in the science fiction *genre*—so he had a first-hand knowledge of of the world of *The White Sheik*. Fellini also supported himself by doing caricatures, at first making the rounds of local restaurants. At the end of the war, he specialised in selling personalised souvenirs to the American servicemen who flooded Rome. The caricaturing almost certainly helped to develop his eye for faces. In addition, observers have reported that he likes to sketch and do watercolours while shooting his films. Apparently these activities aid him in putting his ideas into a visual form. In 1943, Fellini met Giulietta Masina while she was playing the role of the wife in a radio series he had created. They were married that year, not realising that Giulietta would continue to interpret and actually inspire some of Fellini's future characters.

It is impossible, however, to evaluate the full impact of Fellini's personality upon his films. Although much of the enormous volume of published material on Fellini consists of interviews, first-hand reports by people who have worked with him, and his own writings, these sources regularly contradict each other. As Angelo Solmi[12] points out, there is a Fellini legend and the director frequently realigns his life story to conform to it. This seems to be part of a general desire to give interviewers and journalists the kind of answers they want and expect. Occasionally, Fellini will mock a writer who proposes a complex interpretation of a detail in a film or who prods him to dissect *minutiae* from an early work. Yet he is readily accessible to those who want to talk to him and, for the most part, his attitude toward interviewers is resigned and submissive. This tendency to take the path of least resistance is reminiscent of Marcello, Guido and Moraldo. Because of the discrepancies in Fellini's elucidations of his work for the public media, it is advisable to take the films at their own value rather than to try to adjust their implications to bring them into line with the statements he hands out to reporters.

In recent years, partially in reaction to his enormous popular success, it has become fashionable for critics to speak disparagingly of Fellini, denouncing him as repetitive and self-indulgent. A commonly-raised criticism is that Fellini's personal concerns and obsessions are of little relevance to the contemporary cinema in an era of social upheaval. This reasoning is a descendant of the belief that all the resources of the motion picture should be mobilised in support of today's critical political and economic struggles. If one feels compelled to enforce a limited role upon the cinema, this line of thinking may have some validity. Otherwise, it makes as little sense as the accusation that Fellini was a "traitor"[12] to neo-realism because he reduced his interest from the masses to the individual.

In *Roma* Fellini shows himself in conversation with advocates of two

opposing ideologies. First a group of students challenges him to give his
film an "objective point of view" and to deal with the problems of "real"
society, of the students and of the workers. Then a conservative older man,
a lawyer, pleads for a glorification of the spirit of the traditional Rome.
Fellini listens politely without really answering either party, and then continues to portray the city in terms of his own experiences and feelings.
Fellini looks quite ill at ease in this sequence. It is as though, while not
wanting to offend either of the speakers, he is bored by the arguments he
has heard a hundred times before. Much of his discomfort is evidently due
to a feeling of being trapped. Regardless of the alternative he selects, some
segment of the public and critical community will be outraged. So, char-
acteristically, Fellini opts for the course which is most personally agreeable
to him. There is a suggestion here (as in Guido's reaction to the reporters'
question in 8½), that a person cannot become politically involved without
at least beginning to come to grips with himself. Such a concept may well
be petty and self-centred and certainly does not justify Fellini's seeming
disinterest in the world beyond himself. But while we cannot condone his
lack of social commitment any more than we can approve of Marcello's
treatment of Emma, we can understand it, just as we understand the relationship in La dolce vita.

In making films that draw heavily upon his own past and feelings, Fellini
is dealing with the material he knows best. He has frequently turned down
period pieces and films about non-Italian subjects on the grounds that he
could not adequately treat something with which he is unfamiliar. "How,"
he once wrote, "could I make a film in America without knowing the country backwards? I wouldn't feel ready to make a film in America unless I
knew what coloured tie was worn by a lawyer in Boston or how a prostitute
talks in Cincinnati . . . How could I start shooting a scene in a New York
restaurant at 4:30 in the afternoon if I have to rebuild the atmosphere in a
studio? I can't depend on others."[44] Since 8½ he has maintained a base of
fantasy in his films which allows him to be inaccurate or illogical with im-
punity. In Satyricon, admitting that he didn't know the first thing about
the customs and behaviour of the ancient Romans, he forsook historical
verisimilitude altogether, giving his imagination free rein to make everything as strange and unrealistic as possible. By avoiding subjects outside
his range of experience Fellini has undoubtedly spared himself potential
disasters along the lines of Antonioni's Zabriskie Point. Fellini has never
lived in abject poverty or been the victim of political persecution; he is
neither a sophisticate nor an intellectual. His vision covers a very narrow
segment of the universe, but within those limits he has great depth of feeling and perception and an awesome ability to express them on film.

The fact that Fellini uses his life as a point of departure does not necessarily limit the scope of the film or its relevance to the viewer. The in-
scription on the American poster for 8½ is, of course, absurd: "This film
talks about you," it reads, "about your life . . . about your family . . . about
your work . . . about your doubts . . . about your dreams. You will see your-

self in the leading role as though you were looking in a mirror. This is your film." Nonetheless, in the same way that the paralysed girl in *Il bidone* makes Augusto think about his own failure and moves him to cheat his colleagues, Guido's inability to get along with other people may prompt us to ponder the dissatisfaction in our own lives. The specific problems of Guido/Fellini are unique; his state of mind is not. And since Fellini is most adept at conveying a state of mind, it serves as the common ground on which Fellini and his films meet and engage the viewer. Even films with pat *dénouements* and unusual circumstances, like *La strada* and *Juliet of the Sprits*, generate genuine (as opposed to conditioned) emotions, to which most spectators can easily relate.

Fellini's films stress sensation. They are conceived primarily in terms of reaction rather than narrative. This principle is illustrated by an early scene in *Roma* in which a family is shown in the local cinema gazing in

open-mouthed, bug-eyed wonderment at the "spear and sandal" epic on the screen. Here, in a single image, is the effect that Fellini strives to obtain in his films. If he can hold his audience spellbound, dazzle them, or leave them with a surge of exhilaration, then he has achieved an important success. While this effect is not the sole measure of Fellini's cinema, it is a major concern in *La strada* which leaves the audience with a haunting melancholy, in *8½* with its spirited extravagance, in *La dolce vita's* frenzied richness and in the robust exuberance of *I clowns*.

The creation of such feelings through visual stimuli is very close to what as has been called "pure cinema." But Alexandre Arnoux emphasised the necessity of some coarseness or impurity to bring the viewer into contact with a "pure" work.* This is one count on which Fellini, in his great enthusiasm, has occasionally left himself vulnerable—especially when he becomes overly enamoured of his ability to create bizarre private worlds through the camera. These spectacles may be "pure" in the sense that they can exist only in the cinema, but unless we can relate them to something in our real world, they are meaningless. This required taint of ordinariness is what Arnoux meant by "impurity." *Satyricon*, for example, is hallucinatory from start to finish. Its characters, settings and events are all too far removed from us to produce a reaction even in a surrealistic sense. It belongs exclusively to the imagination of one man, and the rest of us can view it only with clinical passivity. Our impression of Trimulchio's banquet, say, is merely one of size and strangeness. The film comes to life only during the "minotaur sequence," the picture's sole subjective passage, because we are made to experience Encolpio's fear and bewilderment. *Juliet of the Spirits* radiates erotic splendour in the visits to Suzy's house and explosive horror in the gathering of the demons (a scene that is every bit as effective as the surprisingly similar moment in Bergman's *Hour of the Wolf*). But the massive scale of these segments overwhelms our feeling for Giulietta and her personal and marital difficulties. The film is splendid as exotic spectacle, but because its anecdotal component frequently gets lost in the spectacle, it is difficult for the viewer to "make contact" with the film—to relate parts of it to anything he understands. Hence, the phantasmagoria sometimes seems gratuitous and indulgent.

The charge that Fellini is tiresomely repetitive is quickly refuted by contrasting his individual films with one another. Almost any film-maker with substantial control over his work will return to the same themes and *motifs*. But in terms of format and style, Fellini's cinema is in a continuous state of growth and evolution. Certainly the presence of a single consciousness can be detected throughout Fellini's work, but one could hardly claim that any two Fellini films are even close to identical. Among his later films (the ones that are most often assailed by critics who fault him with duplicating his own work) *La dolce vita* bears little resemblance to *8½* in either structure or atmosphere. And while *Juliet of the Spirits* deals with a marital

*Clair, René, "Cinema Yesterday and Today." New York: Dover, 1972. p. 99.

problem like the one in *8½*, it does so from a point of view that is neither male nor egocentric. Giulietta's sensibilities are quite different from Guido's or Luisa's. Furthermore, *Juliet of the Spirits*, unlike *8½*, runs its entire course in a fairy tale milieu. *I clowns* is designed as a pseudo-documentary to answer a question that Fellini poses regarding his own filmic style. *Roma*, on the other hand, is a series of free reminiscences through which Fellini reveals his attitude toward certain changes that have affected his life. *Fellini: A Director's Notebook* has several segments which appear in expanded versions in *Roma*. *Director's Notebook* was made for American television, presumably to give viewers an impression of how Fellini makes his films and where he gets his ideas. In the film, he visits the "night people" in the Colosseum and then shows the "Man with the Sack" sequence that was cut from *Nights of Cabiria*. It was in the Colosseum, he explains, that he originally met this strange philanthropist. By the same token, the traffic jam in front of the Colosseum and the views of Rimini are simply sketches for a film he has in mind. They are valuable because—after *Roma* was released—they show how Fellini eventually elaborated those germs of ideas into complex set-pieces.

One reason for the accusations of redundancy that have been leveled against Fellini may be the way some of his set pieces resemble one another. But even those set-pieces with identical premises have different meanings and effects in different films. Both *Toby Dammit* and *Roma* contain rides on the Raccordo Anulare highway. But the trip from the airport in *Toby Dammit* is a procession of macabre sights as seen through the eyes of the drugged actor. These views are mostly amusing, and they follow one another leisurely, without the mounting fury of the Raccordo Anulare sequence in *Roma*. In *Toby Dammit*, the ride is just another incident in a train of supernatural events; in *Roma*, it has its own angry mood and becomes a chaotic nightmare, completely out of control. The *Roma* sequence actually exhausts the viewer with images and cutting that are much too ferocious to be merely diverting as in *Toby Dammit*.

It is true that evocations of Fellini's boyhood occur in *8½*, *Roma*, *I clowns* and *Amarcord*, but each instance is original and tailored to the specific intentions of the film in which it is found. The flashbacks to the farmhouse in *8½* are meant to give us a taste of the safeguarded quality of life that Guido desires. The conflict between the "purposeful" rigidity of the Catholic school and the "temptation" of Saraghina lets us in on the origins of the Carla/Luisa conflict. In *I clowns*, the survey of Rimini's human oddities furnishes a rough base for the comparison of clowns to people, the major theme of the film. To this end, many of the people— especially "Big John," Giudizio, the *vitelloni* and the coachmen—have an intrinsic pathos that makes us like them in spite of their unorthodox appearance and deportment. Others, including the stationmaster, the mutilated war veteran, and the midget nun, seem unbalanced and threatening, like the clowns that frighten the child Fellini. The provincials in *Roma* are played for their sense of self-importance. Fellini finds it funny that

these small town types think they are the focus of the universe. Their conceit becomes even more absurd against the pictures of the teeming city
that follow. *Amarcord* represents a hardening of Fellini's attitude toward
these people as he recognises the roots of Fascism in their smallmindedness.

Fellini's films document his progress from provincial obscurity to international stature. Since leaving Rimini, he seems to have changed through
a process of assimilating deeply felt experiences, rather than through any
sort of intellectual broadening. His morality is based upon an intuitive
sense of what people need, of what makes them happy. His cinema, then,
has become, first and foremost, a cinema of pleasure and emotion. It is
immaterial that his ideas are far from complex or profound. Richness of
expression and intensity of feeling are the qualities that make his films
exceptional.

2

A World of Symbols

There is a distinct tendency to over-read symbols in Fellini's work—to hunt them out consciously, define them and arrange the rest of the film around them. This method of interpretation may be applied with limited success to the few films which are not about particular individuals—*Roma*, *I clowns*, *Amarcord* and perhaps, *Satyricon*. In all other cases the approach is misleading since Fellini's symbols depend upon context and are not always consistent within a film, or from one film to the next. It also distracts the viewer from the human enrichment that is gained by following the experiences of his characters. The meaning in Fellini's films is found in the lives of the characters themselves; the symbols are there only to help us achieve a deeper appreciation of these lives.

Symbolic potential is an important consideration in Fellini's selection of settings, but it is most definitely not the only one. Consider, for example, the penultimate sequence of *Nights of Cabiria*. On the eve of their marriage, Cabiria and Oscar walk through a forest toward a high cliff overlooking the sea. It is nearly dusk and Cabiria is quite contented with her new situation; her gait is light and she darts about gathering flowers and chattering happily. They arrive at the precipice where the sea, magnificently reflecting the last rays of the setting sun, is spread out beneath them. It is here that Cabiria learns that her intended is interested only in robbing her. He grabs her purse and stumbles away through the woods.

Mere description cannot begin to convey the horror and pungency of this episode. Its impact is the concerted effect of at least three levels of visual and associative meaning. At the surface is the narrative function of the image and sound. We see the two people walk to the scene of the crime, hear Cabiria talk about her experience with Giorgio, watch her come to the realisation that she has been duped, and witness the purse snatching. It is a dramatic and shocking climax to the story. The reversal, however, is not entirely unexpected. The wood through which they walk is dense and dark. The trees are uniformly straight and so tall that their boughs are above the upper boundary of the frame, leaving only their trunks visible. This sinister atmosphere is reinforced by the way the camera observes its

*Setting for atmosphere: Oscar (François Périer) betrays Cabiria in beautiful but
ominous surroundings at the end of NIGHTS OF CABIRIA.*

subjects from the far side of a line of trees. The periodic passing of a
trunk between the couple and our eye is psychologically disturbing and
underlines how physically isolated the pair are at that moment. By creating
a foreboding atmosphere, the stroll in the forest gives us an understanding
of the action beyond that supplied by the narrative. It is an ominous prelude to the betrayal.

One might reasonably accept the forest, with its identical parallel tree
trunks, as symbolic of the monotony and lack of genuine human contact
in Cabiria's life. Then the geography—the fact that the forest ends at the
top of a sheer bluff—intimates that her "walk" with Oscar will lead to a
dead end and cannot take her away from the conditions which she ardently
hopes to escape. The scene, then, has symbolic and metaphorical, as well
as narrative and atmospheric, significance.

The second phase of this passage is equally multi-layered. Their destination has an eerie beauty which produces a mixed reaction in the viewer.
Cabiria, still trusting, is enthralled with the scenic display. Its warm radi-
ance might be a manifestation of her own happiness. But a long shot sil-
houettes the prostitute and her companion against the sky and water, showing that Cabiria is in a potentially hazardous situation. At this point we
become certain that Oscar is going to make his move, and the landscape—
without changing physically—takes on a bizarre, nightmarish aspect, unlike

any view in our real experience. The sudden transformation is as devastating as the jolting turn of the narrative. It becomes impossible to look at the site with the glowing wonderment felt upon first glimpsing it.

As Oscar makes his getaway, the sun has almost sunk beneath the horizon, bringing the night and casting a chill over the scene. Even though it is a summer evening, the temperature seems to drop twenty degrees. To extend the connotation to metaphor, the opportunity Cabiria has counted upon to bring about a change in her life has disappeared like the sun. She is left, temporarily, in a state of darkness and despair. But the corollary to the onset of darkness is that the sun must eventually rise again. As if to confirm this, she soon finds herself in the midst of a group of youngsters who are singing and enjoying the mild night. The warmth is returning and her mouth broadens spontaneously into a smile. We assume that the teenagers will lead her out of the forest.

The ending raises some general points about Fellini's use of locations as keys to a sequence. First, the presence of the forest is in no way strained or artificial. It is a real forest and a logical place for *fiancés* to take a walk. In spite of its importance to the construction of the passage, no effort is made to distract us into a consideration of its significance. Many viewers may not even be aware of the couple's surroundings but will respond, at a pre-critical level, to the darkness of the place and to its seclusion and claustrophobic uniformity. The wood, when properly photographed, provides the exact overtones that Fellini desires. The same may be said of the spectacular view from the cliff and the use of the sun to communicate the cyclic nature of Cabiria's rapidly fading joy. The choice of setting allows the basically tragic anecdote to end on an upbeat note. Although Cabiria has just suffered a traumatic disappointment, we know she will be happy again in the future, if only fleetingly. We are reassured that this woman for whom we have come to care is, indeed, all right.

Events in Fellini's films always transpire in the most appropriate of all possible environments—those that facilitate the mood and emotional content of the action. Cabiria's betrayal could have taken place in an alley at noon without changing the gist of the story. But the harshness of such an arrangement would stress the cruelty of the deception rather than the spirit and resilience of the victim. A change of place, even at the very end, could send the film off in a completely different direction.

As we have seen in the example of Cabiria in the actor's apartment, it is not always necessary for a place to be in harmony with a particular individual in order to impart information about him or her. The dwelling is a reflection of the actor's tastes and style of living, so Cabiria's relationship to him is identical to her relationship to the *décor:* they are frankly incompatible. A character may even be alternately concordant and discordant with a single setting, as in the music hall sequence of *Nights of Cabiria.* At first the camera shoots from the stage into the darkness above the heads of the music hall audience. So Cabiria, under the spell of the hypnotist, waltzes across a black screen, bathed by the warm glow of a single spotlight. She is very much at home in the romantic dream induced by the trance. Then, suddenly, a reverse angle reveals her in relation to the amused crowd and the stage personnel, reminding us that her reverie is artificial. If the two shots seem to contradict each other, it is because the first captures Cabiria's state of mind, typically romantic and optimistic. The second is an objective appraisal of the little dreamer's position in the real world. Generally, in Fellini's films, if a character has *rapport* with his surroundings, they provide an insight into his frame of mind. When he is in conflict with the world about him, our view of him may be either subjective *or* objective.

A perfect demonstration of how the unity between character and setting can help define a state of mind is provided by the scene in Fausto's bedroom near the beginning of *I vitelloni*. The room provides a wealth of information about its occupant; it is both a reflection of his character and a summation of the influences that made him that way. It can be cause and effect concurrently because it is a materialisation of the qualities which, in the small town, are eternally self-perpetuating. Indeed, the room has an old-fashioned look to it and shows signs of aging in a few corners (like the peeling lining of the dresser drawer). The calendar on the wall has had all its leaves turned over and is obsolete. The *décor* and furnishings represent various aspects of Fausto's life in the village. The bed is covered by a wildly flowered spread, typical of the ingenuous aesthetic sense which embraces floral patterns as a basic form of beauty—a sense which is seen again in the boys' admiration of the statue they steal. The blossom *motif* is continued in a religious picture of the virgin and angels which hangs above the bed. The print's presence among other, more prosaic scenes—an oval frame containing a provincial snowscape, a reproduction of a crowded painting, a number of picture postcards and a frame full of snapshot mementoes—is a reminder of the entrenchment of religious values in Italian life in general and Fausto's family in particular. The room looks very much like that of a teenage boy. The same sort of observations could be made about Leopoldo and Alberto's homes. The characters are inseparable from their environment and this bond makes it easy to understand why the *vitelloni* feel no inclination to break with their way of life. When Moraldo finally leaves, the receding shots of the townspeople have the effect of a recoil from the burst of energy he has used to free himself.

In *I vitelloni*, the town matches the title characters, and their complacency is thus linked to the traditional trappings of provincial life. In *La strada*, Gelsomina has a mystical correspondence to nature which reveals her total innocence. The weather always anticipates her moods. And while she is happy in the summer and becomes withdrawn and near death in the winter, the context of the film makes it seem as though the seasons are changing in sympathy with her condition, rather than the other way around. This communication with the elements tells of her purity, metaphorically describes her mood, manipulates the film's atmosphere and facilitates and intensifies our sharing of her feelings.

Gelsomina is the most concerted and uncorrupted instance of the con-

The sea provides a perfect backdrop for Wanda's fantasy in THE WHITE SHEIK.

nection to nature which occurs in all of Fellini's character oriented films
(i.e., those through *Juliet of the Spirits*). In each film the circumstances of
a given character's life dictate the extent to which he is or is not in accord
with nature. Thus Cabiria and the *vitelloni* are more in harmony with the
fundamentals of nature than Guido or Marcello. This can be better understood through a short study of the way Fellini uses the sea, the most consistent representation of this natural state to appear in his films.

First we might conjecture about the sea's significance to Fellini himself.
Since Rimini is a coastal town, the easy access to the sea that it provides
undoubtedly played an important part in Fellini's childhood. This hypo-
thesis is supported by the physical arrangement of the village in *I vitelloni*
and by Fellini's memories of the real Saraghina.[3], [12] It is not far-fetched to
propose that, in his thinking, Fellini links the sea with the relatively free
and secure period of boyhood. Fellini left Rimini for Rome and we see
that in two of his most urban films, *Roma* and *Il bidone*, the sea is not
glimpsed at all. In *La dolce vita* and *The White Sheik*, one arrives at the
sea only after much travelling and effort. Quite possibly, Fellini feels that
his own change of scene, accompanied by an increase in maturity, sophistication, cynicism and the demands made upon him, has taken him farther
away from the sea. Admittedly, this is a very speculative framework, but it
seems consistent with his films. Gelsomina is his most childlike creation

The sea: it is an embodiment of Gelsomina's innocence as well as a medium of continuity in her life (above, from LA STRADA), while (below) the protagonists of I VITELLONI are surrounded by the sea which Fellini seems to identify with his provincial boyhood.

and she is closest to the sea. Wanda's infantile dream world takes its material form at the seaside. In *Amarcord* the entire town takes to the water to
witness the passing of the "Rex" which, to their naive thinking, represents
the greatest excitement life has to offer. When Guido, who idealises the
comforts of his childhood, escapes the traffic jam in his dream, he flies out
to the ocean. When the sea figures in Giulietta's visions of characters from
her childhood, it is serene, blue and sparkling. But in her inhibited state,
as an adult, she dreams of a stale, green sea that yields up a barge of
wasting horses. Augusto, the most hardened of Fellini's protagonists, dies
on a barren rock hill which is the very opposite of the sea. This relationship between physical distance from the sea (or degree of harmony with it)
and a character's psychological, moral or philosophical complexity, is the
only dependable correlation in Fellini's employment of the ocean setting.
The importance of the sea, then, lies not in its absolute symbolic implications, but in the relationships that various characters have with it.

    La Strada contrasts the relationships that the two principals maintain
with the sea. When the pair stops by the sea after leaving Rome, Gelsomina
delightedly rushes to the shore and stops there, radiant with pleasure. She
asks Zampano the direction of her home, not because she is homesick, but
because the view reminds her of where she used to live. Nature, and the
sea in particular, is the medium of continuity in her life. Just as she was
unconcerned that she would not witness the growth of the tomatoes she
planted—after all, flowers and vegetation are part of a single great continuum—she doesn't care about the number of miles to her mother's house

*The sea harbours the illusions of the town in AMARCORD as the populace set
out to catch a glimpse of the ocean liner "Rex".*

or whether they are travelling toward or away from it. The fact that there is no interruption between the spot upon which she stands and the shoreline that runs past her former home gives her great satisfaction. Zampano, on the other hand, wades brashly into the tide, oblivious to the beauty of the site. This is a powerful, physical demonstration of his insensitivity and, not surprisingly, his companion is soon infuriated with him. "You're a beast," she yells. "You have no feelings."

Here, one character is in concordance with the sea and the other is not. The body of water serves as a dividing line between Gelsomina and Zampano in much the same way that the apartment sets up a border between Cabiria and the actor. The sea is like an extension of Gelsomina and Zampano's matter-of-fact attitude toward it reflects the way he thoughtlessly takes his companion for granted.

In the end, when the news of Gelsomina's death finally penetrates Zampano's callousness, he returns to the sea. At first he repeats his earlier movements, tramping into the water and washing his face. But when he looks at the sky and his laboured breathing turns to sobbing, he collapses to the ground as the camera cranes upward, isolating him on the beach. The sea now acts as an agent for Gelsomina (or perhaps, in the broadest poetic sense, it is the other way around), fulfilling her "purpose." Becauses of his experience with her, Zampano has finally felt emotion and come back to the sea. His position before the sea differs markedly from Gelsomina's earlier posture of serenity and confidence. At the edge of the sea, Zampano is isolated and lost. But the endless lines of waves gently lapping the shoreline offer a kind of comfort. It might even be said that the sea is now in sympathy with him. After this moment he can never be the same person he was before. This experience on the beach represents both a termination and a start for him, much as Cabiria's last betrayal, within view of the sea, marks the end of one cycle of her life and the beginning of another. The presence of the ocean with its eternal rhythms gives the final shot an eloquence and poignancy which goes far beyond the emotions stirred by the event it depicts. In addition to its narrative, atmospheric, and metaphorical meanings, the sea is used as a poetic *motif* in this case.

La dolce vita contains a slightly different example of two antithetical relationships with the sea. At the film's conclusion both Paola and Marcello are in apposition to the sea. Paola, the young girl seen earlier at the café, is the film's only unimpeachable character. She is actually a positive symbol, a counterpoint to Marcello and his associates. As a reminder that some people and things remain uncorrupted, she serves as the film's credential of constructivity. Her freshness complements the clean breath of air we feel when the participants in the "orgy" emerge at dawn into the new morning and walk to the coast. Like Paola, the sea is robust at that moment, having vomited up the ugly, rotting ray fish. She calls to Marcello, but the noise of the waves prevents her from being heard or understood. The perplexed Marcello gestures apologetically to her across the short stretch of

The city: EUR, the showpiece of fascist architecture, is the site of Mazzuolo the censor's battle with the giant Anita Ekberg. From THE TEMPTATION OF DR. ANTONIO.

water that separates them. Then, turning his back on both Paola and the sea, he rejoins his debauched comrades. The sea is vigorous and congenial to Paola. It has a protective, cleansing quality which keeps her free and vital. Conversely, from Marcello's side, it is a barrier turning him away from the ideal which he has sought throughout the film. In preserving Paola, the sea acts in much the same way as at the end of *Satyricon*, where it provides Encolpio with a route of egress from the decaying nation. Both young people are in tune with the water.

The sea, the woods, nature in general, the actor's apartment and Fausto's room are all parts of a commonplace universe which unobtrusively co-operates in establishing appropriate moods for the films. In turn, these surroundings acquire new colour and meaning from the people who pass through them. But the external world in Fellini's films is not always so passive or obliging; at times it is actively hostile and confining. When a character is either oppressed by or a child of our sophisticated, technological age, he tends to gravitate toward the artificial and mechanical. Steiner and Mazzuolo (in *The Temptations of Dr. Antonio*) are both frustrated by contemporary society (albeit in different ways) and both reside in EUR. Giulietta, the ideal wife, is virtually a prisoner of her comfortable, modern, sterile house. Trimulchio, a leading citizen of a culture even more decadent than that of *La dolce vita*, presides over a monstrous dining hall. Often the automobile and highway, perhaps this century's most visible and omniscient

articles of technology, become a cage as in the dream at the beginning of
8½, on the Raccordo Anulare in *Roma* or in *Toby Dammit*. As Fellini has
become increasingly preoccupied and distressed by the challenge of achieving inner contentment in modern society, such gaudy and elaborate settings
have come to dominate his films and overpower his characters.

One of Fellini's most distinctive matchings of place, event and personality is the introduction of Steiner in a modernistic EUR church. At first a
church seems an unlikely place for a meeting between Marcello and Steiner,
but this is far from an ordinary house of worship. Its *facade*, constructed of
glass and bleached-white concrete, is bleak and rectangular. Even the winged
statuary above and to the sides of the entrance seem to have been cast as a
single piece with the building. The architectural severity is continued inside by the sanctuary's vast open spaces and monotonous angularity. Behind
the pulpit, beneath a steep arch, is a huge, shiny spherical sculpture. The
entire design seems far removed from the structure's intended spiritual
function. Atmospherically, the church is cold and empty. At this point we
know of the emptiness that Marcello feels in his life, so these surroundings
suit him perfectly. Because we discover Steiner within this hollow mountain, we infer that he exists in an identical spiritual void. While in the
church, both men seem to have a common position and point of vantage;
they are both small and isolated in the expanse. This is a point that might
easily have been missed if our initial contact with Steiner were at the gathering in his apartment where, surrounded by his family and at home with
well known intellectuals, he seems to occupy a very different universe than
Marcello. The church meeting gives us a feeling, perhaps even a premo-
nition, about Steiner; without it we would be hard pressed to make sense
of his subsequent murder-suicide.

That which we sense about Steiner through the atmosphere of the cathe-
dral is conveyed implicity by Fellini's choice of location and handling of
space. This process is roughly equivalent to the way we feel anxiety when
Cabiria and Oscar take their walk through the forest to the cliff. And in
the same way that we are offered the setting sun as an elucidation of Cabiria's position at that moment, Fellini overlays our intuitive grasp of Steiner
with information communicated via a more explicit metaphorical mode.
But this time the outcome of the metaphor is frustration. The unusual
organ, the "voice" of the church, is also Steiner's voice. Steiner spontaneously plays a few notes of jazz until the priest casts a disapproving eye on
him. The short burst of frivolity is obviously a natural form of expression
for Steiner, an entirely effortless action on his part. Like the priest, however, who professes a liking for jazz before he dampens the recital, we can
see that the music is entirely inappropriate in the forced solemnity of the
church. So Steiner lowers his mood and, concentrating intensely, begins to
play a sombre fugue. He restrains and modifies his lighter temperament to
meet the demands of the situation. Later on we watch him play host to a
party of pretentious intellectuals. Here, too, Steiner is out of his natural
element, but because he carries the title "writer" he must adapt himself to

this society, even at the cost of his personal satisfaction. At one point in the organ loft scene, Steiner invites his friend to try his hand at the keyboard. Marcello obediently tries a couple of notes and gives up. He doesn't know what he wants to play and is, indeed, unsure whether he can play anything at all. In any case, he knows he could not match Steiner's proficiency. A reflective, unhappy expression crosses Marcello's face as the music commences. Steiner plays his fugue fluently and mechanically, but Marcello does not discern that while the piece is right for the setting, it is absolutely wrong for the soloist.

Although the idea of the church holding Steiner at bay is as ingenious as it is expressive, it still follows the rule that metaphors, in Fellini's films, are not to be dragged in just because they provide a convenient means of commentary. Fellini justifies the use of the church, on narrative grounds alone, by making EUR Steiner's home and having Steiner obtain a scholarly book from the priest. The abruptness that might be expected in suddenly introducing a location that will not figure in the later developments is completely mitigated by the film's episodic construction. Moreover, the look of the church is compatible with the look of the film: a shifting landscape of old and new as established in the opening sequence with the helicopters. But the most important point of all is that the church and the rest of the neighbourhood are contributing causes of Steiner's dilemma. A man in Steiner's predicament could only exist in the shadow of an EUR or its equivalent.

In *La dolce vita*, as well as other Fellini films, the directionless commotion of Rome goes hand in hand with personal confusion. The city is at the far end of the line from Rimini and the sea, and it offers none of the stability of rural or small town life. In *The White Sheik* and *Variety Lights*, the protagonists are country people who have no intention of maintaining permanent ties with Rome. They are buffeted about by forces that they can never hope to master; but finally they leave or go home, completely unchanged by the experience. In these cases the city is a counterpoint against which certain of the characters' qualities become evident. The Rome of *The White Sheik* is constantly changing. The streets are being torn up by hammer wielding workmen and a marching band appears out of nowhere, nearly trampling Ivan Cavalli. This chaos is a far cry from his mania for organisation and scheduling. Even the police station, the foundation of order, is a nightmare of dusty files, towering stairwells and inquisitors with rattling typewriters. The city's massiveness and population density undermine his air of self-importance. A similar debunking occurs in *Variety Lights*. As long as the troupe is on its backwoods touring route, Checco has some stature as a performer and schemer and as the object of Milena's affections. But as soon as he hits the city and goes to the haunts of the show business people he is eclipsed by "artistes" who are more successful than he. The sly wickedness of his flirtation with Liliana instantaneously pales against the perversity of the night-club crowd and their quadruped dancing.

The city: in the big nightclub, Checco (Peppino de Filippo) and Liliana (Carla del Poggio) move from provincial conceit to a more embarrassing position. From VARIETY LIGHTS.

The city: Cabiria (Giulietta Masina) watches the fire breather as Ivan Cavalli (Leopoldo Trieste) sulks in the background in THE WHITE SHEIK.

At this point it should be emphasised that while Fellini frequently uses the city to supply an ambience of confusion and corruption, he is under no obligation to attach the same connotative meaning to the metropolis every time he uses it for a setting. The scenes of wartime Rome in *Roma*, the opening panorama of *The Temptations of Dr. Antonio* and the range of location and associated mood in *Nights of Cabiria* (from Via Veneto to Ostia) affirm that Fellini sees Rome as a richly varied place. Because he is attracted to richness (rather than decadence as many people seem to believe), he frequently shows us these other sides of the city. Even in *The White Sheik* and *Variety Lights*, a shelter from the uproar of the city can be found late at night in the empty piazzas. In the latter film the squares provide the simple and free spirited "eccentrics" with an opportunity to take over and express themselves. Even the policeman who, in other circumstances, might be expected to quash the performance, enjoys and approves of Moema's singing.

The versatility of the city as a metaphor is impressively demonstrated in *Il bidone* which offers a view of Rome that is 180 degrees out of phase with *Variety Lights*. In *Il bidone*, the sidewalks always look warmly alive with people. This bustling crowd seems very willing to assimilate Picasso and Iris as they stroll along with it. But Augusto looks like an outsider when he manoeuvres himself along these same streets. It doesn't matter what the city could offer him; he has picked his life and goals and grown old with them. Unlike Picasso, we never see where Augusto lives. It is too late for

The city: Fellini fears the new forces which are eradicating the life he once knew in Rome. He would like to preserve the human spectacle of the music hall audience (above), but the ancient city is being taken over by sinister, technological powers which are embodied in the metaphor of the goggled cyclists. From ROMA.

him to recover the roots he has abjured, so he can do little more than wander aimlessly among those who are more fortunate, looking for his "big deal." He is boastful or at ease only in the café where he tries to sell a watch to another con-man, at the night-club and during Rinaldo's party. In the tranquil night-time streets which offered a respite to Cavalli and Checco, Augusto spews forth the unhappiness and resentment that have been seething inside him.

It is crucial for Fellini's characters to prevent themselves from becoming fixed in relation to the material world around them. If they capitulate to their surroundings, they forfeit their precious individuality and moral independence, and are lost. This is the direction in which Marcello is heading at the end of *La dolce vita*. It is also the trap that has caught Steiner. Guido's optimistic reverie begins only after the workmen have started to dismantle the scaffolding, freeing his life from the rigid monetary and concrete production concerns that have restricted his ability to deal with his problems. By leaving home, Moraldo prevents himself from turning into merely another unit in the repeating pattern of provincial life. The characters for whom there is the most hope are those who prevent themselves from becoming stagnant, objectified or backed into a corner; they are the ones whose universe is the most changeable and varied: Gelsomina's life has the endless variety of nature. Cabiria ultimately finds herself permanently removed from her former neighbourhood. After Giulietta frees the spirit child, she emerges from her house into what looks like a completely new world.

Roma is the logical conclusion of the ascendancy of technology and full-scale chaos in our cities. It is only in the wartime recollections that individuals seem to matter. The visit to the *pensione*, the *trattoria*, the music hall, and the whore-houses are virtual cavalcades of memorable faces and personalities. They emphasise the lusty vigour and diversity of the population—the people themselves are the spectacle. The only characters in the film (excluding the part in Rimini) to be given extended treatment appear in these sections. In the morass of the Seventies Fellini despairs of finding beguiling prostitutes, pretty German girls or blustering, scatalogical masters of ceremonies. The surrogate for young Fellini in the Forties sketches seems much happier and more relaxed than the Fellini we see following the camera vehicle on the highway, shooting in Piazza Ste. Maria en Trastevere, or being "harassed" by students. In contrast to the views of the past, the Rome of today appears to have been commandeered by machines and faceless crowds. The main attractions in these set-pieces are not people, but traffic jams, mobs of demonstrators and "hippies," and a motorcycle gang. The goggled, leather-clad cyclists who are impossible to tell apart and seem to form a single unit with their vehicles, are the last word in the supplanting of individuals by mobs and machines.

Fellini's concern that his characters not become immobilised and "typed" by their surroundings carries over to the way he uses people as symbols.

While there is an allegorical level to some of his films, his characters are still, first and foremost, human beings, worthwhile in themselves. Except when he is dealing in broad satire, as in *Toby Dammit* or *The Temptations of Dr. Antonio*, they are never subservient to the demands of the allegory. Even the minor functionaries who are required to represent certain values and ideals, are given full status as complex men and women. Like locations, the people in a Fellini movie must have a justification other than their values as symbols.

The final shot of *I vitelloni* is the boy with whom Moraldo has often spoken, seen from behind, balancing on a rail as he walks back to the train station. He has just seen Moraldo off and the departure scene serves as a coda in which the boy acquires a new significance. He is Moraldo as a child, the young man who perennially inhabits villages like Rimini. Moraldo has just taken a big step, hopefully toward the maturity that has escaped Fausto and the others. As Moraldo the Man leaves in search of new possibilities, Moraldo the Boy stays behind. This ending has numerous implications: it reinforces the drastic nature of Moraldo's break; it confirms the timelessness of the events we have been watching; it lends a delicate, nostalgic flavour to the departure. But it is only in retrospect that we see the youngster as a full-blown symbol. In his first late night meeting with Moraldo, he already has a definite charm and spontaneity. We might easily feel some apprehension at this point that life in the town and contact with the *vitelloni* will sap his freshness. He also plays an important role in developing Moraldo's inclination to leave. The mere fact that the boy works for the railroad turns

Characters as symbols: at the end of I VITELLONI, the boy walks back to town along the rail, thus becoming a symbol of Moraldo's boyhood in the never-changing town.

Characters as symbols: Peter Gonzales in ROMA represents young Fellini freshly arrived in the city.

Moraldo's thoughts toward going away, just as seeing Fausto off on his honeymoon did. When he tries on the boy's railway cap, he sees some of himself in the youth who will grow up in Rimini. The impact of the boy upon us and the film is out of proportion to the size of his part.

When Fellini assigns a meaning to a character, in addition to his intrinsic value as an individual, that meaning will usually fall into one or more of four categories. First is the person who acts as a stand-in for Fellini—the autobiographical character. Although Peter Gonzales in *Roma* is never directly referred to as "Fellini," there is no doubt as to his identity from the moment he steps off the train at the station. The hat he wears and the narrative are clues. But his modern hairstyle and way of dressing, as well as his relative detachment from the frenetic activity around him, conclusively single him out as the agent of Fellini's memory. In *8½*, Guido's life does not match Fellini's event for event, but there are enough coincidences to ascertain that the real and fictional directors are of the same stock. Even if Fellini had attempted to disguise these points of similarity, he would inevitably have imposed his own feelings as a film-maker upon Guido. Marcello, in *La dolce vita*, is not Fellini in the literal sense, but his way of reacting and his general discontentment with himself reflect Fellini's feelings. Sometimes Fellini will parcel out his own characteristics to several people in a film. He has, to varying degrees, put a portion of himself into Fausto, Alberto, Riccardo and Leopoldo, although Moraldo, as the most observant and dissatisfied member of the group—and as the one who actually leaves town—is the chief Fellini stand-in. It is not essential for a character to bear an historical or physical resemblance to the director in order for him to embody some of his fears and obsessions. Augusto, for example, personifies Fellini's anxiety about aging, a theme that has held a prominent place in every Fellini film since *Il bidone*.

A second way of making people into symbols is to use them as mirrors that give the main character a glimpse of himself or a part of himself. To the objective spectator, these people are physical externalisations of the protagonist who clarify—or re-state in new terms—some of his feelings or circumstances. The boy in *I vitelloni* falls into this group. Furthermore, if we arrange our perspective on the film so that Moraldo is its focal point (this is simply one of many permissible, non-exclusive approaches), then the other *vitelloni* also function in this manner. As Moraldo watches them, he becomes progressively more disenchanted with the rut he shares with them. While he often feels a tinge of disapproval at the way his friends conduct their lives, he recognises that their follies and misadventures are just the active stage of his own moral apathy. The unflattering impressions of his own existence, as reflected in the lives of his comrades, strengthen his decision to leave.

A third variation is the person who stands for a particular vocation, mental disposition, or class of people. The producer, the starlets, Daumier and the agent in *8½* belong under this heading. They all have well defined roles in the development of the film, but they are also employed toward a satiric end. In the same category, but a step above the producer and company, are the Cardinal, Guido's parents, Carla and Luisa. They represent conflicting influences that continually make demands of Guido. In *La dolce vita*, almost everybody except Marcello stands for a particular sector of society. Each is a prospective solution to Marcello's quest to give substance to his life, and each is shown to be unsatisfactory in one way or another. Steiner, the intellectual, commits suicide—perhaps because his discipline has brought him to an unbearably harsh vision of the world. It is easy to understand how horrible such a vision might be when it is unredeemed by the simple human values and faith that his intellectual society ignores or stifles. Maddalena, despite her immense wealth and "jet-set" status, is a bored and voracious nymphomaniac. Sylvia, another of Fellini's earthy, sexual creatures, cannot be confined or controlled. Emma offers Marcello the "perfection" of bourgeois marriage, but her nagging and possessiveness repel him. His father, the product of the existence Marcello abandoned when he left his provincial home, is naive, unfulfilled and pathetic. His heart condition restricts even his smallest attempts at pleasure.

The fourth type of Fellini character-*cum*-symbol is the man or woman who is the embodiment of an ideal. These people are, at once, the most abstract and the most concrete of Fellini's human symbols. Paola, for example, is the only one of Marcello's acquaintances who has a mollifying effect upon him. At the café, Marcello is so taken with her that he comes

Characters as symbols in 8½: Pace (Guido Alberti, extreme left) is Fellini's vision of a producer, while the American woman (Gilda Dahlberg) is the epitome of the movie fan magazine writer.

out of his irascible mood and even phones Emma, almost apologetically. In this scene we discover a number of facts about Paola: she is from the provinces; her working father left her near Rome and she is homesick; she would like to learn to type; she likes music; she hopes that she will soon move elsewhere. These bits of information give her a past and a future, bringing her to life. This background is very important because ultimately she will be used to persuade us that the goal Marcello has given up on is really attainable. Therefore, we must think of her as a real and plausible person. If she were nothing more than an abstract symbol, her appearance at the end would be unconvincing and seem like a facile attempt to vindicate the preceding three hours of cynicism and desolation.

In *8½*, Daumier criticises the "girl in white" in Guido's scenario as being just such an abstract, ambiguous symbol. In doing so, he lays the basis for the character Claudia. In his fantasies Guido can get everything he wants from the spectre of Claudia—affection, devotion, sex, motherliness, understanding, etc.—with no obligation or return on his part. But when he is confronted with the real Claudia—or at least the actress whom he has chosen as the incarnation of his abstract fantasy—it is obvious that only an imaginary phantom can fulfil these needs while meeting his egocentric terms. As they drive to the springs, the corporeal Claudia refuses to indulge Guido's confession of desperation and need for salvation. When he asks

Characters as symbols: above, the three principal characters in LA STRADA have allegorical significance but, below, their symbolic connotations are secondary to their humanity—the murder of Il Matto (Richard Basehart) evokes a terror that goes beyond a mere symbolic death.

if she could give up everything and devote herself to the one thing that could give meaning to her life (meaning himself), she counters by asking if he could do the same. All along she continues to ask for an explanation of her part in the film. When the car pulls up to the *chateau*, Guido's mind conjures his personal "Claudia," who lovingly greets him at a table set for two. At this point it is clear that there is an irreducible gap between what Guido wants and what he can expect from a real woman with her own needs and sensitivities. The difference between what Guido selfishly believes he should have and what he might possibly attain among real people is the same as the difference between Claudia in her abstract and concrete states. Claudia has no sympathy for a man who cannot or will not return love. Guido runs through his customary rationalisations about why he (in the guise of his pet character) will not give of himself to the woman who might "save" him: "because he doesn't believe her," "because it's false that a woman can change a man," "because I don't want to film another lie." But Claudia, the actress, flatly dismisses each one by insisting that the real problem is that he "doesn't know how to love." Because of Claudia's dual nature as a person and a symbol, it is dramatically permissible for her to state the problem frankly, whereas the other characters only talk around it.

In outlining four convenient categories for the symbolic treatment of people in Fellini's films, I have emphasised the way that symbolic meaning is found in conjunction with human values, rather than at their expense. These four connotative standards can, themselves, be interrelated in a single character who displays several of them simultaneously. The connective mechanism involved is often a shift in our way of viewing the character. For example, to Fellini, the *vitelloni* are a mosaic of himself in his early years. From Moraldo's subjective point of view, his friends have their greatest impact as reflections of his own wasting existence. Objectively, we are most impressed with them as being characteristic of provincial life. This structure is like a set of Chinese boxes. Our objective assessment recognises all three meanings and Fellini's experience encompasses that of Moraldo.

The most intricate interplay among various levels of meaning and points of view occurs in *La strada*, where the three heroes are indisputably characters in an alegory. ~~Gelsomina is innocent, natural and trusting—man in his in an allegory.~~ Gelsomina is innocent, natural and trusting—man in his most childlike state. Zampano seems exactly the opposite, cynical, callous and selfish. They epitomise two conditions, two states of mind, two types of people. Il Matto is easily recognisable as an embodiment of faith. He is first seen on his tightrope, wearing a pair of costume wings, high above the festival crowd. It is a religious procession that leads Gelsomina to the site of the performance, and when Il Matto dies he assumes a crucifixion position. He has a mystical gift of prophecy—"Zampano will live a long time," he tells Gelsomina, "I'll die soon." His pebble speech is actually an article of faith, something to justify Gelsomina's life. Because of it, Gelsomina stays with Zampano and finally, albeit posthumously, is responsible for changing him, for bringing him closer to humanity. The moral of the allegory, then, concerns maintaining a belief in one's self and a receptiveness to others.

If one combines the adjectives I have used to describe Gelsomina and Zampano—innocent and cynical, callous and sensitive, selfish and loving— the result is a reasonably good description of two of Fellini's most autobio- graphical characters, Guido and Marcello. Both of them have all of these qualities to varying degrees, and the internal conflicts they cause are partly responsible for the two men's difficulties. This line of reasoning helps to explain what Fellini meant when he referred to *La strada* as his "most auto- biographical film"[28] and "the complete catalogue of my entire mythical world, a dangerous representation of my identity undertaken without pre- cautions."[28] In *La strada*, several characters divide the properties of Fellini's self-image. The conclusion of the *La strada* allegory is the basis of some of the problems posed in *Il bidone, La dolce vita, 8½,* and *Juliet of the Spirits*: those which involve striking a balance between responsibility to one's self and responsibility to others. Giulietta measures her own worth in terms of what she can give to Giorgio. Augusto, Marcello and Guido are at the other extreme, egotistically failing to acknowledge their obligations to everyone else in their lives. There are echoes of Zampano and Gelsomina in such Fellini couples as Marcello and Emma, Guido and Luisa, and Giulietta and Giorgio.

La strada's classic form and moral do not diminish or eclipse the innate importance of the characters. At times Fellini enforces this importance by letting our feelings for the characters conflict with the best interests of the allegorical treatment. The emotion we feel when Il Matto is murdered is much more profound than mere intellectual regret at seeing a positive sym- bol destroyed. This is partly because we experience the event subjectively— like Gelsomina—as well as from an objective angle which favours the alle- gory. Also Fellini combines Il Matto's symbolic properties with whims and contradictions that give him weight as a complicated human being. Far from being a run-of-the-mill Christ figure, Il Matto is often malicious in his pranks. He is certainly not passive or submissive as witnessed by his attempt to smash Zampano with the tyre iron. The grossly symbolic com- plaint that he voices on the verge of death—that Zampano has broken his wristwatch—has a materialistic ring that goes against the spiritual solemnity this moment would have if it transpired on a purely allegorical plane. Just before the killing it is even possible to feel that Zampano's anger is justi- fied. After all, there are indications that Il Matto has always been the one who provoked their skirmishes. At the end, we feel sadness because Gel- somina is dead, not joy over her allegorical fulfilment. We have shared too much with her to accept her death simply as a sacrifice to the requirements of the moral lesson.

The most important products of Fellini's work are the thrill or emotion that it gives the public and the solicitude it generates for his characters. Symbols that demand a rigorous, rational interpretation contribute little to these ends. So when Fellini does offer a symbol as key to a film it is almost always calculated to make its point by striking a psychological nerve deep within the spectator. His symbols are aimed more at creating an effect than a concise statement of meaning. This principle, of course, has some of the hazards of a filmed Rorschach test in that people with different backgrounds and emotional make-ups will respond differently to a given visual provocation. The situation is essentially that encountered in watching many surrealist works. If, as it has been maintained, the only possible explanation of Buñuel's *Un chien andalou* would be a psychoanalytic one, then it must be obtained by analysing the individual reaction of each viewer and not by tagging Freudian implications onto each image. When applied to Fellini's work, which is not predominantly surrealistic, the principle is still effective and his symbols often affect us profoundly on a private level. What is lost in expressive precision is more than compensated by the gain in total impact. Also, Fellini has several ways of reducing the amplitude of the variation in individual response. He has often stated that he makes films for "like-minded men" and we can infer that he uses himself to gauge how other people who see his movies will be affected by a particular object or situation. The reaction of the natural audience for his films should not vary enormously from this self-determined basis. Then, by making his symbols exceptionally bizzare, he further assures that he will elicit a strong response from the major portion of the audience.

In addition, Fellini's symbols are not strictly irrational, but hybrids, with both intellectual and emotional content. At first we react to them without really knowing why. But in afterthought, we can usually find some kind of logical basis for them within the framework of the film. The famous airborne Christ, for instance, provides a startling, explosive opening for *La dolce vita*. In the first shot, the Christ statue, hanging from a helicopter (which looks rather like an ugly insect) sweeps past the ruined aqueducts, structures of antiquity. The figure is then carried past several new high-rise apartment buildings, including some under construction, then over a rooftop patio and towards the Vatican. At one point, a solitary worker waves at the statue; at another a crowd of men and boys on the ground chase it, shouting excitedly. St. Peter's Square, in the aerial view, is teeming with people. Just by itself the picture of Jesus and the aircraft is weird and unnerving. And the shots of him moving through the air, not far above all that human commotion, gives the impression that a far-reaching apocalypse is imminent. As has been noted, this prologue also sets the tone of the movie, progressing from the ancient aqueducts to the ultra-modern blocks of flats—a panorama of architectural confusion. Upon reflection, we can easily put this event into metaphorical terms. The most literal reading would take it as the suspension of moral values by a cold, technological age. Another translation might see it as an elusive symbol of serenity and self-contentment passing over the troubled city, just out of reach. This interpretation would be particularly suitable, for Marcello is following the statue. In the broadest sense the vision is emblematic of a society in flux. Yet, despite this multiplicity of meanings, the sequence's primary power is in the way it sets up shock waves of disequilibrium that penetrate the entire film.

The symbol that ends *La dolce vita* has a similar dual nature. The fish

Symbols with multiple meanings: the helicopter with the Christ statue which opens LA DOLCE VITA (above) and the strange fish which closes it (right) are symbols that work on both an intellectual and an emotional level.

certainly stands for the shapeless, decaying society that the film has explored, and for Marcello, degenerately stuffing himself with pointless pleasures. But these interpretations would not make much of an impression upon us where it not for the mixture of repulsion and morbid fascination that the animal inspires. Small arachnids have already begun to eat its rotting flesh and the fisherman's comment that it has probably been dead for several days heightens our disgust. The image is so vivid that we can almost smell the creature. All this makes Paola's subsequent appearance that much more welcome and refreshing by comparison. It is as though Marcello has been given one last chance to renounce the desperate hedonism he has embraced and resume his efforts to find meaning in his life. For Marcello, the fish—its mouth crammed with jellyfish that it never managed to swallow—should be an object lesson in the consequences of pursuing his present course. That he can turn his back on Paola after being confronted by the monstrosity gives us a frightening understanding of how absolutely he has abandoned hope. The close-up of the beast's dead, glazed-over eye—which seems to stare at both Marcello and the audience—becomes a challenge to us, one that we dare not refuse.

Fellini frequently uses a modification of another standard surrealist technique, that of taking an object out of context and making it stand on its own. This forces us to assess our attitudes toward it, and brings to light aspects of it which are otherwise hidden. Again, the opening of *La dolce vita* is such a case. The idea of a celestial God descending from Heaven loses its awesomeness when we see his representation gliding through the air. Although we still recognise that the statue is a symbol of faith, while dangling in tow beneath the helicopter it looks ridiculously inadequate for all the things that Christians expect of such a figure. The new perspective is consistent with the different metaphorical interpretations of the scene and with the themes of the film. Civilisation itself has grown in such a way that it is refractory to archaic, dogmatic religion. The hope that Marcello is pursuing is a false one; he needs to look, with honesty, to people for his deliverance. Thus Paola becomes a countersymbol to the flying Christ.

The statue's new meaning is the result of its being thrust into a situation

completely alien to the way we are accustomed to thinking of it. More commonly, Fellini will take an object and transpose it to a context that is actually more appropriate than the one in which we normally find it. Toby Dammit's Ferrari—with its grille approximating a snarling mouth—is discovered beneath Klieg lights, surrounded by mist and under the guard of a shadowy man. It looks desirable, mysterious and meanacing. This portrait is more than a crystallisation of Dammit's delirium; it is a snide, satirical comment on the way people idolise this kind of vehicle. In the new context the absurdity of this mystique is self-evident and so effectively presented that few people could comfortably shrug it off.

The method of altering context is similarly used for satire in *The White Sheik*. An entire romantic mythology is irreparably fractured when its constituents are shown dealing with the petty concerns of the real world. Oscar, Felga and their veiled associates are not exactly awe-inspiring as they dance, eat lunch, exchange dirty jokes and ride in the back of a truck. Fernando Rivoli may be the perfect glamour figure in the pages of the *fumetti*, but to those involved in the hard, commercial side of the papers he is unprofessional and an annoyance. In a real boat or atop a genuine camel, his legendary command of the sea and desert disintegrates. If anything, his awkward seduction attempt marks the erstwhile romantic symbol as even more incompetent than the ordinary mortal. The harder he tries to maintain the illusion of the White Sheik, the more effeminate and unheroic he seems. Fellini completes the metamorphosis of context by picturing this title character as a hen-pecked husband. He still possesses all the virtues of the "White Sheik," but now they are seen in a different light. Any respect we may have had for these qualities, or the man who embodies them, disappears in laughter as Rivoli rides away, clinging to his leviathan spouse.

Occasionally, Fellini will inject a seemingly extraneous element into an otherwise straightforward sequence. I am thinking particularly of the horse that walks by Gelsomina after Zampano has gone off with the redhead. While this embellishment's relationship to the action may not be immediately clear, it is so in tune with the mood of the scene that there is no question of its appropriateness. As Gelsomina watches Zampano drive away with his new acquaintance, she is momentarily puzzled, then crestfallen. Suddenly, in a single night shot, the horse emerges from the foreground and plods past Gelsomina. Then it is dawn. The inclusion of the night shot conveys a sense of waiting which we would not have had, had Fellini cut directly from the exterior of the restaurant to Gelsomina sitting on the roadside the following morning. The horse, with its slow, steady gait, adds weight to the interlude, making us feel the prolonged passage of a finite period of time. It implicitly tells us of the psychic burden Gelsomina bears that evening. This is one of the most daringly poetic moments in any Fellini film. In attempting this effect, Fellini successfully ran the risk of disrupting the flow of surface reality with a visual *non-sequitur*. Although, statistically, the chances of a stray horse trotting down a village road at night may be negligible, the mystical aspect of Gelsomina's presence is strong enough to allow for such a phenomenon. Working in Gelsomina's subjective sphere, Fellini introduces a symbol which, while not wholly logical, is intuitively correct, given the context.

The peacock in *Amarcord* is another symbol that has no precise meaning, but fits perfectly into the film. The brilliantly plumed bird appears unexpectedly in the middle of a snowball fight, its bright colours standing out against the dull shades of the winter day. It might be just another apparition in a town that is encumbered by illusions, but its shrill cry is convincing evidence that it is real. The peacock is a portent; its unexpected arrival has a jarring effect that sets the mood for the death of Titta's mother. Its harsh screech seems to warn everyone to beware of its fascinating beauty.

Fellini's faces: at the shrine of Divine Love, Cabiria is flanked by a number of distinctive individuals. From NIGHTS OF CABIRIA.

3

Spectacle: Magnifying the Personal Vision

Fellini: A Director's Notebook ends with a parade of diverse, eccentric people trying to win the director's attention and, hopefully, a part in his next film. Members of the crowd compete for his time by playing the accordion, asking absurd questions, reading from foreign language newspapers, distributing photographs, flexing muscles and hustling artware. These people's appearances match the outrageousness of their tactics. In body type they range from wiry to ultra-muscular to enormously obese, and from child-sized to gigantic. Their faces, expressions, dress and mannerisms are varied, unusual and striking. Although, outwardly, Fellini has greeted his visitors with an air of boredom and annoyance, he admits that he has a deep affection for them. "I am very fond of all these characters who are always chasing after me," he confides to the audience. "They are all a little mad, I know that. They say they need me, but in truth I need them more. Their human qualities are rich, comic and sometimes very moving."

This manic display is shot from Fellini's point of view as though the lens were his eye. (Once we even see his hands and forearms closing a folder as though he had momentarily glanced down to co-ordinate the movement.) The episode could be described as a "circus," a "fresco" a "sideshow" or even as "a series of vaudeville acts." These analogies give us a key with which to approach the use and place of spectacle in Fellini's films. The scene is typical of Fellini's vision of life and of the human world around him. His final comments on the crowd of prospective movie stars establish a compatibility between his humanistic attitudes and the gaudy exhibitions that run through his work. His words sum up the attraction he feels for the motley crowd of people that move endlessly through his films. From the most peripheral bit player to the central character, Fellini is consistent in his belief that every human life is valuable and interesting.

Clearly, Fellini cannot delve into the life of every extra who passes before his lens. On the other hand, if he were to ignore the minor roles in his movies or slide his extras around the set like so many bodies needed to fill a given amount of space, he would be untrue to his respect for the importance of the individual. We know that Cabiria's hopes are riding on her expectation of a miracle at the tabernacle, but the ritual is surely of equal significance to the other pilgrims. Though our attention is focused upon Cabiria, other members of the procession have features that are distinctive enough to enable us to pick them out from shot to shot. We might settle upon the masculine looking old woman with the scarf wrapped around her head—who is often glimpsed behind Cabiria—and wonder what need has brought her to the shrine. Because we can single out specific people in the procession, we realise that the human current which sweeps Cabiria along is composed of individuals, each feeling the intensity of the moment in his own way. When it is understood that the ritual will cruelly wreck the aspirations of a multitude of real people—rather than just disappoint a nebulous, impersonal mass—the true horror of the activity at the shrine becomes apparent. If Fellini had simply called for a hundred men and women of ordinary appearance to take part in the sequence, we would be less likely to realise that the supplicants outside Cabiria's party also have a commitment to the event. Our recognition of the spiritual devastation inflicted upon each member of the procession galvanises the experience for us.

Fellini uses physical features not to stereotype the members of his supporting cast, but to make them distinctly different from each other. In doing so, he preserves the integrity of the individual and reasserts his own wonder at the diversity of human form and temperament. He has a gift for finding people whose faces and bodies seem to reflect a recognisable personality. In this respect his experience as a caricaturist has served him well. By supplementing the natural endowments of his players with carefully chosen clothes, gestures and posturings, Fellini can convey, almost instantly, a complex impression of a character who is in view only momentarily. In *I clowns*, during the child's approach to the circus, the camera tracks past a woman dispensing tickets from a wagon window. She is dark-haired, round-faced and earthy. Her general appearance and the little bit of spaghetti that she is pushing into the corner of her mouth make her register on our memories and even give us an idea of what it would be like to stand near her. The few feet of film in which she appears make an enormous contribution toward establishing a kind of sweaty, human flavour around the manifestations of the big top.

Fellini effectively applies this method to important supporting characters as well as to the constituents of crowd scenes. *I vitelloni* never explicitly explains Leopoldo's horrified reaction to Natali—nor does Fellini give Natali the limp-wristed movements that traditionally identify homosexuals in movies. Rather, by controlling lighting, dress, and the facial expression of the actor playing Natali, the director is able to arouse our

Fellini's faces: Natali, the homosexual actor, looks quite benign when he first appears on stage in I VITELLONI.

suspicions about the "great artist," but reserve the definitive revelation until the last moment. On stage Natali looks like any other ham actor. He does not seem out of the ordinary until we see him talking to the boys through the torn curtain of his dressing room. Away from the stage lights his make-up and lip rouge transform him into a peculiar clown with white skin and cavernous eye sockets. This shot is the first intimation that something is amiss. Later, a single, short shot clarifies everything. Natali, in close up, cocks his head to one side, raises his eyebrows and, in dulcet tones, asks Leopoldo, "Are you afraid of me?" At that moment the odd smile that we saw in the dressing room appears again. It is fuller than before and the space where Natali is missing two upper teeth (we could not see this space earlier) makes the grin demonic. At the same time, we are impressed by how aged the actor is. In less than ten seconds Fellini has told us much about the man while generating the shock that the sequence requires.

Sometimes Fellini will obtain a specific effect by bringing together many people who share a desired quality. Even then he refuses to amalgamate his subjects into a crowd that presents a single, summated face. The spa

Character and spectacle: the spa in 8½ is revealed on film through a series of complex camera movements which combine panning with tracking. We see the area as if we were accompanying Guido, looking around ourselves as we walk along.

in *8½* is such an instance. The common denominator there is old age, a prospect which Fellini has always treated with both dread and sympathy. The dread is evident in the very infirmity of those who are taking the cure: the man who needs the support of two attendants to get to his chair, the trembling hand of another visitor as he limps along on his cane, the lady with the stringy hair and flat features who has fallen asleep under the hot sun, the toothless gentleman who shields his head with a newspaper. Not all of the faces are desperate, though. There is the *blasé* lady with the cigarette and oversized sunglasses. We also find several women with parasols, looking like friendly grandmothers. One of them even throws a kiss toward the camera. Like the chubby, giggling nun who chortles as she quaffs her mineral water, these women are pleasant, but irritating because they seem out of touch with the world around them—another symptom of aging. The goal of this pageant, in the context of *8½*, is not to comment upon old age but to evoke Guido's impression of a loss of personal prowess by placing him among the old and sick. In doing so, the sequence displays the ravages of senility. At the same time, however, it generates a great deal of compassion for the sufferers—compassion that goes beyond a conditioned response to a pathetic sight. It is the character that Fellini finds in their faces that makes us react to them as something more than living props.

Spectacle gives Fellini a way to magnify the emotion and significance of a life or an event. This effect helps explain the predominance of spectacle in films that are, at heart, intimate portraits of two or three central personalities. His desire to uphold the worthiness of the story's most peripheral figures justifies the extreme individualisation of the many extras Fellini employs. But why, in the first place, must he mount the private lives of Guido, Gelsomina, Cabiria and the others on such a massive stage? Is it really necessary, we might ask, to bring together a hundred extras just to establish Guido's feeling of dessication?

It is important to remember that the films are built around their protagonists. Guido is fully preoccupied with his inability to move ahead on his film and to put his personal relationships in order. This pressing concern pervades every aspect of his life and he finds reminders of his paralysis wherever he turns. The gathering of old, exhausted people at the springs externalises Guido's depression on a grand scale. The spectacle heightens our sensitivity to his feelings, while the enormity of his vision of everything around him enlarges him for us. This does not mean that we are more easily moved by Guido's problems just because they are presented on an

Character and spectacle: Guido peers over the rim of his glasses. In 8½, this gesture usually indicates that the following shot will be subjective.

Character and spectacle: Busby Berkeley's production numbers stress geometricity. From FOOTLIGHT PARADE.

Character and spectacle: although parts of the sequence at the Grand Hotel with the sultan's wives in AMARCORD may resemble Busby Berkeley-like spectacle, this adventure is built from the point of view of Biscein, the liar.

oversized canvas. (As we will see shortly, the effect may be exactly the opposite.) But because his life evinces itself in such imposing patterns, we more readily accept Guido and his difficulties as being worth our attention.

In the same vein, we might dismiss Gelsomina, Fausto, Picasso or Cabiria as small, ordinary, unimportant people who hardly merit our concern or consideration. Yet, our view of them is inseparably tied to high-powered parties and festivities, exotic homes and villas, frightening religious processions and strange night-clubs and entertainments. These individuals are literally enveloped in excitement. Involvement in such gigantic, emotionally supercharged events adds conceptual mass to the characters. The intensity of a spectacular episode clings to the character, strengthening his presence without distracting from the spectacle itself.

If the impressiveness of this sort of sequence is to accrue to a character, however, the sequence must maintain a close relationship to him. A protagonist will reap little benefit, in the way of increased viewer regard, from spectacle that proceeds without referring back to him. Fellini's emphasis upon the subjective pays off handsomely when it comes to tying his characters to various sensational events. Examples from three films nicely illustrate how Fellini uses subjectivity to convert visual exhilaration into significant insight or regard for a character. The sequence at the spa in *8½* transmits Guido's point of view with full force, giving the viewer an idea of Guido's problem as he perceives it. The raucous wedding party in *La strada*, followed by the mystic confrontation with Oswaldo, is a haunting demonstration of Gelsomina's isolation. And the uproar created by the storm at the "Miss Siren" contest in *I vitelloni* leaves us with a sense of the panic and disorder that have just entered the lives of Fausto and Sandra. Each of these examples is an extravagantly mounted set piece which, though stimulating in its own right, adds immeasurably to our familiarity with a character.

All of the cases cited above use a small amount of subjective camerawork to create the primary link between the character and the spectacle. This short footage is enough to diffuse the character's presence throughout the segment. After making provision for this bridge, Fellini develops the spectacle in whatever manner he considers most advantageous. The frankly subjective camera set-ups serve the same end as the shots from behind Fellini's desk in *Fellini: A Director's Notebook*: they establish the correlation between the character and the exhibition on the screen and they remind us of the personal origins of what we are seeing. In *La strada*, the camera sometimes walks in Gelsomina's place as the children lead her to Oswaldo's room. Once they arrive, it tracks in on Oswaldo in his bed. Shortly thereafter, there is a stationary shot from a position near Oswaldo in which Gelsomina approaches him. These shots fully convey the affinity between Gelsomina and the lonely retard. The loneliness embodied in the sequence becomes an important point of reference as we follow Gelsomina's further travels. The intimacy of the Oswaldo episode also sharpens the effect of the preceding wedding feast. There a long, rapid tracking shot reveals the celebrants fighting, eating, throwing food and *confetti*, and chasing each other. The track, so much colder and more impersonal than the near-magical visit to Oswaldo, effectively excludes Gelsomina from the gaiety and camaraderie. Thus a tiny piece of subjective camerawork—as Gelsomina runs after the children—personalises in retrospect what would otherwise seem only a vulgar, but funny spectacle. A more direct effect occurs when Sandra is being congratulated for winning the "Miss Siren" title. The only explicitly subjective work in this sequence occurs as the faces of her admirers are thrust suffocatingly close to the lens. Then the camera suddenly tilts upwards, mimicking Sandra's abrupt fall. Even if one does not immediately guess that her unexpected nausea is a symptom of pregnancy, it is clear that something is terribly wrong. The graphically rendered fainting spell picks up the confusion of the party and the panic created by the ominous storm and focuses them upon Sandra. The wild party then becomes expressive of a huge, personal crisis.

Fellini's emphasis on the personal and subjective aspects of his spectacles endows them with great vitality. It is a remarkable feat, in the first place, to devise something so huge and so out of the ordinary that a person confronted with it will be at a loss as to how to respond. In the cinema, Fellini and Busby Berkeley are the most notable among the few who have had unlimited success with this method. Both of these film-makers have imaginations that operate far beyond the confines of routine human experience.

Both know how to open up their gargantuan constructions gradually, in a way that will milk the maximum effect from them. (Berkeley uses what he calls a "disclosure shot" while Fellini continually adds new elements to his "production numbers.") But, Berkeley's camera positions are dictated by the geometry of the musical routines. Neither his facial close-ups nor kaleidoscopic views correspond to anything vaguely in the "first person." In fact, he reinforces the non-involvement by opening and closing stage curtains on his acts. Fellini's spectacles, in contrast, most often start and/or end with the character concerned. The first shot at the springs in *8½* begins with a short pan from two women walking in the distance to another pair of women, back to back, in medium close-up. The shot continues, following a lady in the background until it comes across an elderly man whom it discovers in the foreground. Somewhere during this manoeuvre the pan turns into a track and proceeds without interruption to a seat where an old gentleman hands a glass of water to a lady friend. Immediately, the camera

Character and spectacle: the fascist wedding in AMARCORD is one of the rare Fellini spectacles (outside of SATYRICON) which bears no significant relationship to a character's presence. The oversized spectacle is meant to look absurd; its geometricity stresses fascism's disregard of the individual.

Character and spectacle: these two stills reflect Marcello's position with regard to the "miracle" in LA DOLCE VITA. Above, the crowd and children are seen in a high angle shot as Marcello watches from atop a scaffolding. Below, at another time Fellini tracks, at a steady velocity, along the line of the sick and crippled—the tracking is a clinical and dispassionate way of observing the hysteria.

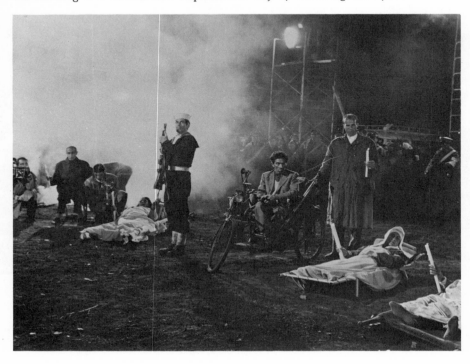

picks up a priest who emerges in the distance behind the chair, and tracks him until he disappears behind a group of white-hatted grandmother types, one of whom throws a kiss toward us. Then, without pausing, the camera moves to take in the nearby orchestra conductor. We can easily make a case for this travelling shot as a subjective rendering of what Guido sees while he walks toward the women dispensing water. In any case, the definitive subjective moment occurs at the end of the segment when Guido fantasises Claudia at the water dispersal counter. This flight of imagination indicates that Guido is the instigator of the spectacle we have just seen.

Unlike Berkeley, Fellini reveals his spectacles in a way that imitates our natural attentive processes, concentrating, if only briefly, upon one element at a time. We tend to notice moving things more readily than stationary ones, so that if something moves across the camera's field of view—the priest in the spa sequence, for example—Fellini will zero in on it. If someone pops into the frame from up close, Fellini almost reflexively shifts the centre of interest to him in the same way that our eyes adapt and readjust when we realign our gaze. So the camera behaves as if it were our own organ of vision under our own control. In the sequence at the spa, it is not until we have had a chance to wander about in this manner, picking up details for ourselves, that Fellini puts everything together with a long, high crane shot. Since we have seen the spa (or Guido's vision of it) as we would if we had been there ourselves, the experience is more immediate than if it were offered as a passively-viewed, Berkeleyesque phantasmagoria.

The camera style in the spa sequence filters the experience through a kind of funnel of subjectivity. At the widest end of the cone are the panoramic vistas like the crane shot and the shots where people walk toward a fixed camera. These give us a broad idea of the arrangement of the space and action. The effect of these views is modified by the feeling of having discovered much of the area ourselves—a "viewer subjectivity" resulting from camera movements which simulate our own system of gathering information. At the neck of the funnel are the shots which are subjective from Guido's point of view, and which relate the total spectacle to him. So Fellini immerses us, at first hand, in the staggering spectacle and then leads us to transfer the impact of the experience to our feelings for his main character.

Fellini has a basic procedure for simulating viewer involvement in the disclosure of a spectacle. He reveals one detail after another, taking care to provide a medium of continuity between the details. The continuity may come from camera movement, a strong sense of place and time, or various rhythmic qualities— both internal (especially cutting tempo) and external (music, for instance). When we survey a complex space or event we can concentrate on only one thing at a time. If we are startled by something in our peripheral visual field while concentrating on something else, we can turn our attention to the new stimulus. But we cannot, simultaneously, continue to view the first item. When several activities are shown in depth in a single frame, the spectator may choose both the order in which he scrutinizes the components and the amount of time he devotes to each.

While this generates a useful visual ambiguity, it removes the man in the theatre seat from the action by a degree. His position is relatively objective and he must act upon the shot—that is, break it down—before he can begin to assimilate it. By providing a governed flow of material, Fellini can guide the viewer's attention, controlling what is seen and the weight given each element. The perception process is included in the film, and like everything else that is projected on the screen, it is magnified, strengthening the viewer's sense of participation.

Most often, the camera movement that supplies continuity between various elements of Fellini's spectacle is the pan. The pan is a natural, quasi-anatomical movement that is the equivalent of a person turning his head. It places the viewer in the centre of everything and can even be used for character subjectivity. When a character's identification with spectacle is unusually strong—as in *8½* and *Juliet of the Spirits* where spectacle is a manifestation of the interior state of the protagonists—the pan is the dominant camera movement. The harem fantasy of *8½*, with its many players and unceasing movement, is handled mostly with pans and variations of pans. Sometimes the camera placement coincides with Guido's position, as during the argument over Jacqueline in which, from a low angle, Fellini pans back and forth among the hostile females. At other times, the effect of head turning is retained although Guido is obviously not the originator of the movement. One such instance is the combination of pan and tilt employed as the women parade their master around the room on a sheet. The camera is actually tracking back in front of the procession. At first it is trained upon Saraghina, who talks about the straightness of Guido's legs; then it pans to the right and tilts downward to look at Guido who is riding close to the ground. Finally, reversing the tilt and panning even farther to the right, it settles on the French actress as she accuses the master of the harem of being a hypocrite. These manoeuvres are natural and help to keep the sequence in the present tense for the spectator. Shortly thereafter, when rebellion breaks out, there are a number of blindingly fast pans in rapid succession. Our eyes would normally conduct themselves this way in a room where a great many things are happening at once. The more studied shots scattered throughout the daydream—the girl with the star shaped hat in silhouette with Guido and his whip visible over her shoulder, or the woman who enters the frame from in front of the camera—do not interfere with the effect of the pans. In fact, they introduce visual excitement of their own, which is swept into the momentum generated by the pans. Many of the other spectacles in *8½* and *Juliet of the Spirits* including the farmhouse memory and the visits to Suzy's and Bishma's, rely upon panning to put the viewer in the middle of everything.

Long tracking shots are also used, at times, to develop viewer involvement. They are most effective in achieving this goal when the character concerned is walking and the shot gives the perspective of a moving observer (the spa sequence of *8½* might serve as an illustration). But when

Character and spectacle: at the end of LA DOLCE VITA, Marcello is totally immersed in pointless pleasure-seeking. Appropriately, the party as the villa is the only sequence in the film to make extensive use of pans.

the character is not moving, the outcome of a track during a set-piece is altogether different. The idea, as with the pans, is that the viewer's relationship to the action should correspond to that of the main character. When the character is not in motion, tracks seem much colder and more clinical. Thus they are ideal for situations where the character is on the outside of the spectacle. In most of Fellini's films the bond between character and spectacle is so substantial that pans predominate. But in two films, *La dolce vita* and *Satyricon*, the characters are estranged from the world around them. The hysteria caused by the "miracle children" in *La dolce vita* is captured in a series of long tracking shots which move at a steady velocity. During the mayhem, Marcello is perched atop a high scaffolding. As he looks on unemotionally his alienation increases; the frenzy of the faithful is certainly not the answer or meaning that he has been seeking. The tracks more than adequately cover the event and convey the horror and madness that permeate it. But the mechanical execution of the shots prevents the impact of their content from affecting our view of the dissatisfied gossip journalist. In *La dolce vita*, tracking shots are used to enforce a psychological distance between Marcello and the spectacle he witnesses. But the "orgy" sequence after Marcello has finally given himself to the debauchery about him, is loaded with pans which put both Marcello and us in the centre of the party. The technique makes us aware of Marcello's full immersion in this loose society.

It might be argued that closed rooms, like the farmhouse in *8½* and the villa at the end of *La dolce vita*, lend themselves to pans, while the wide open spaces of the field where the virgin is seen or the Baths of Caracalla would more readily accomodate tracking shots. Though the principle itself has validity, it would seem that the same considerations that dictate the dominant camera movement would also influence the choice of setting. Surely, it would have been possible to conclude *La dolce vita* with a party in the woods outside the villa—or even with an entirely different sort of revelation. But at that point, Marcello should be surrounded by the pleasure seeking to which he has capitulated. Both pans and an intimate environment are indicated here. Also, we find pans used in several exterior sequences of *8½*—including Saraghina's dance and Maya's performance. Marcello's place in the scheme of *La dolce vita* prompted Fellini to use both tracks and open spaces, while four-walled enclosures and panning generally—but not always—make the most sense for the more private, mentally interior *8½*. Similar reasoning can be applied to the suggestion that tracks predominate in *La dolce vita* and *Satyricon* because the anamorphic process is more amenable to tracks than to pans. In both films the hero is threatened by an all-encompassing, morally degenerate society. Scope provides the best aspect ratio for expressing the magnitude of that menace. Both Encolpio and Marcello (at least at first) are transients in their respective cultures— living in the society while not really being part of it. The feeling that they are "just passing through" is accentuated by the long tracking shots which provide a constant sensation of forward movement. The wide image graphically contrasts the dimensions of the protagonist with those of the society, stressing the great distance that must be covered if the hero is to escape its sphere of influence. So in *Satyricon* and *La dolce vita*, scope and tracking shots are complementary solutions to a single problem of expression.

Satyricon is more dependent on tracks for the disclosure of spectacle than any other Fellini film. Reduced to its simplest terms, *Satyricon* follows a young man whose passionate, sincere love for a boy is the antithesis of the inhumane, pleasure-crazed world in which he lives. Through a series of gargantuan spectacles, the film demonstrates the emptiness and cruelty of this empire until Encolpio bodily escapes from it, boarding a boat to an unknown destination. *Satyricon*, unlike any other Fellini vehicle, is not really concerned with the personal dilemma of its central character. Fellini asks us to accept, without question, Encolpio's rather dubious virtue. Then he concentrates upon ancient Rome itself, using the camera as an instrument for scanning a collection of long, imaginative frescoes. The experience is not unlike Encolpio's stroll through the gallery, with Fellini rather than Eumolpo expounding upon the unending cavalcade of strange artifacts. Beyond their meaning as a reference to Encolpio's continuing journey, the

Character and spectacle: the bizarre spectacle of SATYRICON is viewed clinically, like Encolpio's impassive trip through the museum (above). Sights like Trimulchio's baths (below) have little meaning for Encolpio or for us.

lengthy tracks of *Satyricon* recall a guided tour of a museum containing row upon row of exhibits. Although many of these displays stimulate our curiosity, we are hard-pressed to make much sense of them. There are a number of ways to account for this effect, including Fellini's stated intention that the viewer should relate to these Romans as he would to an alien race that he would be incapable of understanding. But, for this discussion, it doesn't matter whether Fellini is trying to give us a detached historian's view of our own crumbling society, or whether the film is presented as it is because the work of Petronius survives only as a fragmented relic. What must be understood, however, is that *Satyricon* differs markedly from the other Fellini films we have discussed in that its heroes are presented to us on the same level as the institutions and spectacles that are shown. When Encolpio and Giton walk through Suburra early in the film, the camera does not track them nor does it track from their point of view. Rather, it is sometimes with them, sometimes behind them, and sometimes in front of them. Occasionally, when the pair is walking slower than the camera is tracking, the frame will pass by them. Then, at a later moment, they will re-enter the travelling frame under their own power. They are as much a part of the landscape as the drunks, whores and herb sellers. In *Satyricon*, then, the tracking shot not only portrays the relationship of the characters to the spectacle, but reflects Fellini's clinical attitude towards both the protagonists and their milieu.

There is one moment in *Satyricon* when the film breaks free of its monotonous tracks and springs to life—the "Minotaur" sequence. Encolpio finds himself thrown, without warning, into a huge gladiatorial arena. Under the circumstances, he would be expected to glance frantically around himself, looking either for a portal of escape or an explanation. This reaction is translated into a sequence of wild pans, endowing the episode with an energy that the rest of the movie lacks. For the first time we become personally involved in Encolpio's predicament; for the first time we understand what the "student" is experiencing. As extraordinary as the other elements of *Satyricon* may be, Fellini's spectacle acquires exuberance only when its correspondence to a central figure (a character, or in the case of *Roma* and *I clowns*, Fellini) is well delineated.

Because spectacle is so much bigger than life, it lends itself to exaggeration—a quality that Fellini frequently uses to a satiric end. The target may be a character, something external to a character, or both; and satire may be either the dominant tone of the sequence or one of several attitudes incorporated in it. But Fellini makes satiric points best when he plays character and spectacle off against each other. Even as satire, *Satyricon* suffers from Fellini's failure (or unwillingness) to provide a protagonist who has more than a single dimension. Fellini's Encolpio is a far cry from Petronius's cynical, picaresque character who was frequently responsible for his own misadventures. It is typical of Fellini to turn the film's Encolpio into a

Character and spectacle: Encolpio (Martin Potter) prepares to fight the "Minotaur" in the only sequence of SATYRICON that really springs to life.

searcher who has some superficial traits in common with Marcello of *La dolce vita*. But in his determination to make *Satyricon* decidedly different from his previous output, the director leaves Encolpio (and Ascilto and Giton, for that matter) as hollow figures, suspended somewhere between the camera and the incredible exhibitions that it records. One senses satiric intent (rather than a simple effort to establish atmosphere) in such sequences as the walk through Suburra and Trimulchio's banquet. But without a point of reference, which would allow us to ascertain the objective of the ridicule, the satire is lost and the set-pieces become just lengthy catalogues of spectacular excesses. It is as though Fellini were creating incidents of degeneracy and absurdity *de novo*, so that he can attack them. He must have been aware of this problem during production when he told Dario Zanelli: "Really, *Satyricon* is an impossible undertaking; I've no idea how it's going to end up. It's a film which has to depend entirely upon fantasy, a fantasy cut off from our world with its taste for autobiography. It's a species of nebula, and nourished on nothing: because I don't want to make a film that is archaeological, or historical, or nostalgic . . . On the other hand, I don't want to do Petronius either; how can you satirize a world you don't know? Satire makes sense only if it's applied to the world you're in contact with. Could you do a satire on Martians?"[29]

Spectacle as satire: Mazzulo, the would-be censor, is totally inadequate against the giant Anita Ekberg, the embodiment of all his sexual fears. From THE TEMPTATIONS OF DR. ANTONIO.

I do not want to demean Fellini's goal of describing "the life of the Romans as dispassionately as the life of trout."[29] And I would not claim that an attempt to assemble myths, images and sound into a spectacular ensemble is essentially without merit. In *Satyricon*, however, Fellini failed to find the unifying force that he knew was needed to replace his normal involvement with the characters. Formal devices, like the hallucinatory atmosphere, just do not provide a "fluidity in this series of fantastic inventions, a fluency that will make them credible."[29] It is not that Fellini should avoid experimenting with different concepts and approaches—indeed, he has done so successfully throughout his career. But his intense personal rapport with the people, places and events in his films are the essence of his work. *Satyricon* demonstrates what happens when Fellini's satire, mannerisms and spectacles are not backed up by his wholehearted involvement with what eventually appears on the screen.

Fellini's satire is most successful when he judges his spectacle on the basis of his characters and vice versa. We recognise the mentality of the townspeople in *Amarcord* from the vapidity of their dreams and ambitions. And in *The White Sheik* we realise how really horrific the police bureaucracy is when bumptious Ivan Cavalli begins to look like an innocent victim trapped in a maze of dusty papers and corridors. By blowing up the most elementary fears of Mazzuolo, the outraged citizen of *The Temptations of Dr. Antonio*, and personifying them as a building-sized sex symbol who taunts and threatens, Fellini shows the apprehensions of the censor to be ridiculously overwrought. The usually pompous *dottore* becomes a cowering, defensive runt, totally inadequate before the mountain of sexuality. By inflating Mazzuolo's insecurity, we get a drastically different view of the man than we did when he stormed into the official's office to demand an end to dirty magazines. The result is an acid attack on the bluenoses who were scandalised by *La dolce vita*.

While satire is the thrust of the *Boccaccio '70* episode, it is only one of several perspectives inherent in the spa sequence of *8½*. The spectacle there indicates what is on Guido's mind and the extent to which he feels his exhaustion. In addition, it suggests that Guido, wrapped up in himself as he is, is overreacting to his lethargy. Instead of seeking the source of his sluggishness, he paints himself a hopeless picture of the situation and tries to escape into fantasy. Though respectful of Guido's basic dilemma, Fellini mocks his hero's self-indulgence by escalating the images of old age until their cumulative effect is one of absurdity. The use of Wagner on the soundtrack adds to the hyperbole and parallels the satiric side of the visuals.

Even the satiric facets of Fellini's religious spectacles take on an added strength because of the position of a character within them. The wedding of Fausto in *I vitelloni* has a playful, irreverent tone that undermines the holiness of one of the church's most sacrosanct rituals. This subversion starts with our knowledge of the circumstances of the nuptials and Fausto's attitude toward the marriage. Following the shot of Alberto and Riccardo laughing at Fausto's plight, the solemn playing of "Ave Maria" in the church comes off as ironic counterpoint. The camera movement in this scene is playful and wryly exploits the embarrassment of the trapped bridegroom. Beginning with the face of a weeping woman, the camera tracks along a line of guests until it reaches the smiling, but uncomfortable Fausto. The narration, too, is ironic. "It was a beautiful wedding," says the voice over," even though it was put together a bit hastily." As the

Spectacle as satire: the joking attitude of the vitelloni *undermines the religious seriousness of the church wedding in* I VITELLONI. *From left, Moraldo (Franco Interlenghi), Alberto (Alberto Sordi), Sandra (Eleonora Ruffo), Fausto (Franco Fabrizi) and Leopoldo (Leopoldo Trieste).*

speaker describes how Riccardo sang the "Ave Maria" and made everyone cry, Fausto looks up toward the choir loft, and the camera, craning, lets us follow his glance as we would had we been present. It is obviously Fausto who bears the brunt of this sly sequence.

The pilgrimage in *Nights of Cabiria*, the religious procession in *La strada*, and the "miracle" of *La dolce vita* are deadly serious in their satire of church promoted hysteria. The physical and mental violence propagated by these religious functions is channeled to the viewer through the position of the main character. Cabiria and Gelsomina are uncontrollably buffeted about by the mobs of supplicants which turn into forcefully flowing rivers of humanity. It is nerve-racking to see the innocent, curious Gelsomina swept along helplessly by the current. And Cabiria's traumatic realisation that the shrine is a fraud sends shock waves through the audience. On the other hand, Marcello's distance and journalistic non-emotionality make the miracle even more infuriating than the experiences of Gelsomina and Cabiria. It would be emotionally cathartic if we had a place in the centre of the insanity and could work ourselves into a rage over the hideous destruction as in *Cabiria* and *La strada*. But Fellini and his method of presentation confine us to a clinical viewing point. We understand the horror of the hoax, but remain outside it. We are as angered by Marcello's lack of outrage as by the fiasco itself. Each of these three religious crowd scenes would, on its own, be a substantial statement about the church and its tactics. Given Fellini's practice of using distinctive extras, we would, under any circumstances, appreciate the damage these functions do to so many lives. But it is the presence of the central character that gives each of these sequences its extraordinary impact.

The ecclesiastical fashion show from *Roma* is the culmination of all of Fellini's satiric religious spectacles. Although the church may have failed Fellini and his characters, it has, at least in the past, supported a high society based upon papal patronage—the "black aristocracy." Since the death of Pope Pius XII, this aristocracy has had to settle for patronage by

Spectacle as satire: the ecclesiastical fashion show in ROMA satirises the church's use of aesthetic attraction as well as the dying black aristocracy. The appearance of Pope Pius XII is the last hope for the aristocracy which prospered under this papacy.

less regal Vatican officials. In staging the ornate social event, Fellini lampoons those members of the "black aristocracy" who still cling to the vestiges of previous Vatican favours, hoping that they will someday regain their lost status. The significance of this mesmerising bit of film is clear from the beginning. Fellini is attacking a definite group of people who are recognisable (at least to Italian audiences) down to individuals. And there is little doubt that the apparition that appears at the end, during a paroxysm of genuflection, is Pius XII. The gathering weeps and calls after him because his death marked the beginning of their decline. Fellini focuses on the hostess of the *défile*, an aging, wrinkled princess, full of bitterness and contempt for the rest of the world. The decrepitude of the woman, fantasising in her vast, empty mansion, sets the tone of the passage and makes the aristocracy's efforts to recapture the past seem especially pathetic.

There is another aspect to the satire of the ecclesiastical fashion show, one which has a direct bearing upon the processions in *Nights of Cabiria*, *La strada* and *La dolce vita*. This is the way that the church, while offering little that is of substance, holds its subjects through a kind of aesthetic attraction. We may laugh at the first entries in the ecclesiastical fashion show, but as the raiment and models become increasingly macabre, we become caught up in the spell of the event. By the time the case of skeletons and the giant silver hand glide down the walkway, we are shocked at how we have been taken in by the compelling atmosphere. Fellini is asking us to examine our response to religious pomp and symbolism. The church, he assures us, is even more adept than he at manipulating people through spectacle. Men and women flock to shrines, feast day celebrations, demonstrations of miracles and even Sunday mass because of the carnival-like or theatrical atmosphere.

In Fellini's films the relationship between character and spectacle is a reciprocal one. The character benefits because the spectacle "cracks open" his world for the viewer, making it—and the character with it—seem bigger, more important. The extravagant exhibitions fascinate the spectator and engage his attention and interest for the character. In return, the character vitalises the spectacles. His position with respect to these events gives them a personal flavour which increases the audience's emotional stake in them. The measure of a spectacle's success, after all, is the extent to which it produces emotional excitement in those who witness it.

Ultimately, our reaction to one of Fellini's protagonists depends upon our reaction to the spectacle of his life. If we are not thoroughly captivated by what we see, it is not likely that we will care much about him. To guarantee this enthrallment. Fellini relies upon traditional, tried-and-proven forms of spectacle: the music-hall and the circus-carnival. As long as the director can create a state of wonderment in the viewer and then transfer the feeling to the character, a strong audience response is assured.

Straightforward reproductions of circus and music-hall entertainment often provide enjoyable interludes in a Fellini movie. For its first ten

Character and spectacle: the VARIETY LIGHTS troupe's act is based on an assortment of unusual personalities.

minutes or so, *Variety Lights* concentrates upon an actual performance of the troupe and the reaction of their audience. The good naturedness of this sequence starts the film off in an altogether charming manner. An atmosphere of fun is immediately established; its aura will stay with us even during Checco's periods of despondency. The light, rousing character of the film is maintained by this segment and others like it (including the beginning of the party at Renzo's which Fellini handles with a jaunty touch matching that used to show the artistes on stage.) Because of the light tone, we are never too dismayed by Checco's setbacks. This film's opening is an example of spectacle which, while pleasurable in its own right, has important ramifications for the picture as a whole. The same is true of several of the cabaret scenes (a close cousin to music-hall) in *La dolce vita*: the clown with the balloons would be moving in any case, but his appearance at the "Kit Kat Club" while Marcello's father is straining to have a good time adds a wistful note which instils the episode with just the sense of loss it requires.

The show at the Teatrino della Barafonda in *Roma* would be amusing even without the heckling audience. Although the content of the acts may, today, be appreciated only by Italians—and then only for nostalgic reasons— Fellini has polished other aspects of the programme so that it has appeal for a modern, international audience. The lighting, *décor*, costumes, and personalities have been made especially attractive and interesting, adding much to the rich, overall texture of *Roma*.

Both the *Roma* and *Variety Lights* music-hall scenes reconfirm the desirability of building spectacle around characters. The numbers at the Teatrino della Barafonda and in the different provincial halls in *Variety Lights* are effective because they project the personalities of the performers. In both films, the crowds respond primarily to the performer—not to the act—as is apparent from the personal nature of the heckling in *Roma* and from the ticket-buyers' lecherous admiration of Liliana as she dances in the *Variety Lights* chorus. The importance of personality is unmistakable if one compares Liliana's *début* in Parmasani's company with the routines she used on the road. Despite its hugeness and the number of dancers involved, the Parmasani act is dull and impersonal; it lacks the vulgar robustness of the performances by Checco's group. The elaborate scenery and mechanical devices are of little interest without a strong personality to animate them. Parmasani's show is Busby Berkeley spectacle, not Fellini spectacle. It is diverting for us only because we know Liliana and appreciate her attempts to upstage the star.

The circus routines of the different principals in *La strada* are particularly suited to each of them as individuals. Gelsomina is a clown who, though intellectually stunted, has enormous appeal. Zampano's act is a boasting, brutish exhibition of pure muscle which has meaning within the allegorical framework of the film: he is a strong man trying to break, with a breath

Spectacle as entertainment: this shot, bathed in a striking orange light, opens the music hall sequence in ROMA. Fellini often uses such effects to create visual excitement in his spectacles.

of air, the chains that confine him. Il Matto, in his angel outfit, balances precariously on a tightrope while executing audacious stunts. A single miscalculation in his wild movements— or even a strong gust of wind—might cause him to plunge to his death. In our introduction to the madman, Fellini gives us a taste of the risk that is part of Il Matto's life by making it appear, for a moment, that he will fall from the wire.

From his own experiences with the circus, the popular cinema, the musichall and the night-club/cabaret, Fellini recognises that people put themselves into an emotionally susceptible state when they enter a hall or arena to be entertained. This condition increases Fellini's effectiveness in raising his characters' stock with the audience during moments of spectacle. When the ticket buyer is absorbed and enraptured by the spectacle before him— as in the scenes at the movies in *Roma* and *Fellini: A Director's Notebook*— he will be even more receptive than usual to Fellini's revelations of character. We can observe this heightened vulnerability during moments of relaxation in some of the characters in Fellini's films: Augusto is identified and denounced while taking his daughter to the movies. Cabiria meets Oscar as a result of her adventure in the variety hall. Giuletta's image of her father—an important factor in the psychoanalytic rationale of *Juliet of the Spirits*—is formed mostly from her memories of him at the circus.

The traditional spectacles have also influenced the structure of Fellini's films. Variety shows consist of many acts, one on the heels of the next. The circus not only presents its attractions in rapid fire order, but frequently has several in progress simultaneously. The result is a dense, variegated programme that moves rapidly through a number of different moods and is constantly stimulating. This last line could serve equally well as a description of any of Fellini's films.

The key to the breathtaking pace of Fellini's work is its density—the packing of a wealth of detail and event into the shortest reasonable time span. The films themselves are episodic—the episode being the structural equivalent of a music-hall act. Each episode is internally cohesive, almost a short, self-contained movie. With respect to the narrative, the episodes often have only casual interconnections. They come together in a given film because they have a direct bearing upon the characters. Through these multiple vignettes, we can observe the characters from many different view points, in a variety of humours, and circumstances. So in recalling *La strada*, we think first of Gelsomina, Zampano and Il Matto, then of specific segments of the film—the religious procession, the theft from the convent, the wedding celebration, etc. The end product is a tightly packed collection of many different experiences. Because so many incidents are followed to completion, the film seems more concentrated than if it had a solitary plot which was developed in a dramatically linear fashion. In *8½, La dolce vita* and *Juliet of the Spirits* the concentration effect increases the complexity of the lead character.

Fellini's insistence upon spectacular density is carried through from the practice of building a movie from discreet episodes, down to the level of the individual shot, or part of a shot. If our attention lags—if a shot or sequence is held longer than the time than we need to get everything out of it—we become restless. Such a breakdown in the steady flow of stimulation will kill a spectacle instantly. On the other hand, it would be senseless to overload the film with detail that will be missed because there is not enough time available to take in all of it. The trick—and Fellini has mastered it—is to tailor the length of time that a shot or point of interest is on screen to the time the viewer needs to assimilate it. Fellini's style of moving from detail to detail (discussed earlier) is an ideal way to ration time to each element of a sequence. When Fellini uses a series of relatively static shots, his editing is generally tight, piling the shots on top of each other and giving the viewer a minimally adequate opportunity to react to each of them. When the thunderstorm disrupts the "Miss Siren" festivities in *I vitelloni,* there is a fast montage of different corners of the dance area. It is as though we have glanced quickly in various directions—pausing at each position just long enough to get an idea of what is happening there. The technique is used in *8½* just before Maya's entrance. There we jump from table to table—from Pace and his starlet to Mezzabotta to Daumier and the American writer to Guido to Carla to the French actress and her agent. The combinations of characters involved in conversations are continually shifting and we frequently hear a discussion at one table while the camera views a different table. Each shot is strikingly composed, especially in terms of lighting, so there is a fresh burst of interest on the part of the spectator after each cut. This brief sequence is as dense and entertaining as any passage of its length could conceivably be.

A moving camera gives Fellini even greater control over the steady parade of visions that constitute a sequence. There are two possible ways to do this with camera movement. The first is to shift camera positions, thereby creating a new composition that alters the viewer's perception of the shot. This technique is employed during the carrying of the child Guido to his bed after the bath in *8½*. Initially, the lens tracks the woman who carries the boy to the stairs. As she ascends the steps, the camera dollies through an arc of about 90° and cranes slightly so that it looks up the staircase at the woman and her charge, now visible in silhouette. Abruptly, another woman drying another child pops into the foreground at the foot of the stairs. In a few seconds we have had to adjust to three distinct framings, each of which has a somewhat different effect.

The second way of regulating the flow of attractions with a mobile camera is to let the camera, in a track or pan, reveal one detail after another. When Toby Dammit walks through the Fumachino airport the camera catches, in quick succession, people with masked features in the waiting area, a covey of nuns in the gate area, Moslems prostrating themselves in a departure lounge, a black girl at the fountain who steps back in horror before the advancing camera, a weird-looking man in a wheelchair and other striking faces. The experience—partially a distortion due to Dammit's less than lucid state, but not altogether removed from the feeling one gets in the Da Vinci air terminal—is like a trip through a sideshow. The

Spectacle as entertainment: Fellini keeps the viewer's eye busy by packing detail upon detail in his films. The frame shown here is so visually complicated that there is barely time to take it all in. From TOBY DAMMIT.

visitor is given just enough of a look at each freak to tease his imagination. Then he is hustled on to the next booth before he has a chance to reflect upon the monstrosity and, perhaps, discover its artificiality.

/ To keep his spectacles rolling like a good circus or sideshow, Fellini allots each element just enough screen time to entice us, but never enough for us to study it. The time necessary is relative, of course, and expands or contracts according to the complexity of the item on display, how badly the audience wants to see it and how clearly it can be seen. The frescoes in the Metro excavation in *Roma* pique our interest enough to make us want a long, close look at them. While Fellini grants them substantial exposure, he is always tracking in and out on them. The movement prevents our eyes from settling upon the frescoes, so we are never afforded the definitive view we would like. In one sense, Fellini does this to save himself because the studio-designed wall paintings, when subjected to close inspection, lack the appearance of authenticity. But it is more important that Fellini commonly uses such camera movement to throw our perceptive faculties off balance./(As examples, consider the gathering of the apparitions and other visions from *Juliet of the Spirits*, Via Albalonga after hours in *Roma*, and almost everything in *Toby Dammit*.) The business of shortening the time interval assigned to each detail is notably absent from *Satyricon*. There Fellini is determined not only to expose his grotesque creations, but to devour them as well. The long periods he spends examining the whores, slaves and other specimens of ancient life result in the slower, more deliberate pace of *Satyricon*, as compared to other Fellini spectacles.

No consideration of Fellini's spectacles would be complete without a look at *I clowns*. In that film Fellini examines the basis for his depiction of human life in terms of spectacle. *I clowns* speaks of the director's affinity with the circus and justifies the use of caricature in films that insist upon the uniqueness of each individual.

As the film opens, the boy Fellini watches from his bedroom window as the big top rises from the ground like a huge, inflatable monster. The next day the boy visits the circus, an awesome world unto itself. The rows of red seats are empty, like a movie theatre before its first showing of the day. The atmosphere is a reminder of the break in continuity between the world of the circus (or the cinema) and everything outside it. This ambience creates the vulnerable state of mind already mentioned and we are willing to be affected by whatever we might be shown in this cavern. The ringmaster, director of the circus, enters the vacant structure, dons his hat, winks his eye, and the show begins.

The spectacle, which proceeds act by act, runs the gamut in tone. The amazing strongman is followed by the midget clown who parodies his stunts. Next an element of danger is introduced by the lion tamer and knife thrower. After the burial of the fakir, a silly wrestling match is staged. Then things take an eerie turn with the appearance of the ice-green mermaid and the embalmed Siamese twins. The frequent, sudden alterations in mood are similar to the spectacle lives of Fellini's characters which mix episodes

Clowns: an effeminate Alberto Sordi makes a perfect companion for the carnival head in I VITELLONI.

of lightheartedness with episodes of disappointment, terror and disgust.

Finally, the arena is flooded with clowns, all engaged in different comic pursuits. At a given moment, different pairs of clowns are exchanging hats, playing musical instruments, doing acrobatics, arguing, fishing and trying to drive an oversized nail with an equally oversized hammer. Once we have **had a chance** to note all these activities, new ones are added to occupy our attention. This amalgam of activities is typical of the way Fellini's films add detail to detail. The performers play to the child Fellini, as though he were the only spectator present, just as a film plays to an individual filmgoer isolated in the darkness.

The punch line of the visit to the circus is that the clowns frighten the little boy and make him cry, destroying, albeit not very subtly, the commonly held idea that clowns are either sad or funny. One might argue that Fellini, by thinking of the people in his movies as clowns, is limiting the expressive possibilities of his characters. When the child bursts into tears, Fellini takes a first step in demonstrating that there are other dimensions to clowns beside idiocy and sadness.

Fellini then compares some of the Rimini locals to clowns. He concentrates, to be sure, on the town's more eccentric inhabitants—Big John, the midget nun, the quarrelsome coachmen, the mutilated war veteran and the pompous stationmaster. But at the end of this segment Fellini gives us the inevitable Giudizio, a friendly, gentle, village idiot who goes berserk

Clowns: Gelsomina (Giuletta Masina) is described as having "a face like an artichoke" in LA STRADA.

and acts out a battle whenever a war movie plays in town. The *vitelloni* humour him and enjoy his show, but after a while they take the man aside and offer him a drink. There is real pathos here; the town's loafers, themselves clowns, genuinely care for their slightly mad friend. The people who participate in this touching incident are no less caricatures than the clowns in the circus. Fellini is edging us toward the conclusion that clowns are capable of a wide spectrum of rather delicate expression.

Continuing his argument, Fellini introduces a number of clowns and ex-clowns, some in person and some through re-creations. First is the story of Jim Gillion, an aged, sick clown who died when he sneaked out of the hospital to see Footit and Chocolate's famous act. The old man still looks like a clown because of the chalky pallor of his face, and he spends his final breaths laughing at the legendary performers. The film's account of his death is moving and full of tenderness. Later Fellini re-creates the careers of the famous Fratellini Brothers whose make-up, costumes and routines radiate kindness as they entertain the inmates of hospitals and mental institutions.

The retired clowns who are interviewed, Bario and Père Loriot, seem to have permanently assimilated some of their old make-up into their features. In old age they are weary and even a bit pathetic. Still, the line separating the men from their professional personalities has become indistinct. We understand just how tenuous this boundary is when Charlie Rivel slips, almost involuntarily, into the character of his famous Auguste. The ease and naturalness of the transformation is startling. The point that human behaviour is not far removed from clowns' antics is made again, in a more contrived manner, by the discord at the end of the white clowns' fashion show. Immediately afterwards, the French white clowns, Alex, Nino and Ludo, are shown in their street clothes, engaged in an argument very much like the one that caps the fashion show.

Fellini convincingly demonstrates that clowns can project a full range of human feeling. To caricature someone as a clown is not to stereotype him, but to concentrate his qualities, to intensify him. The concentration effect is useful to Fellini in building the density of his spectacles. Natali, the woman behind Cabiria at the shrine, the lady who sells tickets outside the tent, and all the other characters who must make significant impressions upon the viewer in a short time are, in essence, clowns. Time-consuming character manipulation is unnecessary because these people evoke, on sight, a complex reaction from the viewer.

Fellini's major characters also act as clowns. They are not characterised in the dramatic or psychological sense, for our knowledge of them comes, rather, from observation of their physical traits and mannerisms. Picasso has "a face like an angel" and Gelsomina has one "like an artichoke." Alberto Sordi looks effeminate in *The White Sheik*, where he is a hen-pecked husband, and in *I vitelloni*, where he is basically a "mama's boy."

The two clown types in I CLOWNS are the white clown (left) and the Auguste (right).

The hulking Augusto is as worn out as he looks. The body language of the characters is equally succinct and informative. Fausto does a little shadow boxing step to shore up his vanity after the lady from the cinema rebuffs him. Cabiria's dances tell of her spontaneity and lack of inhibitions. Marcello usually faces a problem by giving a disinterested shrug and Guido frequently clowns like a little child.

Both clown acts and Fellini's films are designed to appeal to our feelings and sense of humour, not to teach a lesson. As Fellini works out the equation between men and clowns he looks at emotional qualities and ignores intellectual considerations. Since his films are concerned with the spiritual, sensual and emotional lives of the characters, this emphasis is logical. By casting his characters as clowns, Fellini is able to approach their needs directly, without reference to the philosophical consequences of those needs.

In his introduction to the Cappelli edition of the screenplay of *I clowns*, Fellini discusses the two types of clowns: the white clown and the Auguste. The supercilious, pedantic, hard-headed white clown is the overreacher of the pair. He demands perfection but his irritating self-righteousness just encourages his foil, the Auguste, to rebel against him. The Auguste is the funny-faced clown with the sloppy clothes—an illogical, instinctive underachiever. Even if he were capable of it, he would have no desire to do anything right. Postulating that the two clowns represent two opposing, elementary attitudes in man, Fellini goes on to classify well known people as either Augustes or white clowns. Thus Pasolini and Visconti become white clowns while Antonioni is a sullen Auguste. Hitler is a white clown and Mussolini is an Auguste and so forth. "The game is so real," Fellini says, "that if you have a white clown in front of you, you are forced to act as an Auguste, and vice versa."[36]

If we apply the game to Fellini's characters, we find that, with the possible exception of Gelsomina and Zampano, none of them is always an Auguste or always a white clown. Around Wanda, Ivan Cavalli is a white clown. In the police station or with his relatives, he is an Auguste. With Sylvia or Steiner, Marcello is an Auguste; with Emma or his father he is a white clown. Augusto is a white clown to his partners, but an Auguste to Rinaldo. Guido is a white clown to his mistress and an Auguste to his wife. We infer a clown's personality from his physical attributes and the part he takes in a given gag. Since Fellini does not definitively characterise his protagonists, we learn about them by observing their physical movements and characteristics, and by noting which clown role they assume in each of a number of episodes.

In his theory of the white clown and the Auguste, Fellini states that the clowns, and the attitudes they represent, cannot be destroyed. Ideally, however, they would be assimilated. "Thus . . ." he says, "the irrational, the infantile, the instinctive would no longer be seen with a deformed eye—the thing which renders them deformed."

"The film," he continues, "ends with the two figures (Auguste and the white clown) meeting and going off together. Why does such a situation move one so much? Because the two figures embody a myth that is basic to each of us: the reconciliation of opposites, the singleness of being."[36]

If we examine the characters who, in various Fellini films, symbolise ideals, we find it difficult, if not impossible, to make the Auguste-white clown distinction. Claudia, from 8½, and Paola, from *La dolce vita*, lack signs of either tendency. Could they be the synthesis of the two poles? The case of Il Matto is even more perplexing. Zampano is a white clown and Gelsomina is an Auguste, but Il Matto seems to play both roles simultaneously. He dresses like an Auguste, but when he is taunting Zampano or giving his "pebble" lecture, he maintains complete control of the situation and is clearly the superior participant. When Zampano reacts to the "madman's" jeers, he suddenly loses the self-assurance of the white clown. But he does not convert to an Auguste; he simply gets mad. Gelsomina accepts Il Matto's philosophy and is uplifted by it—a very non-Auguste response. The confusion that the aerialist engenders in the other clowns who deal with him contributes to his ambiguity as a man and as a symbol. The co-existence within him of the white clown and the Auguste evokes the same ideal as the reunion at the end of *I clowns*.

When we search Fellini's work for this theme—the reconciliation of the Auguste and white clown inclinations—we find it in abundance. The satire of *The White Sheik* is ultimately stringent; the conclusion of *Il bidone* is pathetic and the final episode of *La do'ce vita* is cynical. All these outcomes

Clowns: according to Fellini, the reunion at the end of I CLOWNS represents the reconciliation of opposites.

might be attributed to the fact that the protagonist's experiences have not lead him to assimilate the two clown types. It is obvious that Ivan, Augusto (if he lives) and Marcello have become permanently entrenched in their white clown attitudes and will continue to view those whom they consider Augustes through a "distorted eye." On the other hand, the finale of 8½ is stirring because Guido has accepted, at least tentatively, his own extremes of behaviour and feeling and those of the people in his life. In reality, many of his difficulties will undoubtedly continue. But, for the moment, his vision is clear and he sees his relations and acquaintances not as Augustes and white clowns who will make him their foils, but as people who are important in his life. Giulietta emerges from her bout with the spirits having reconciled two opposites: her Catholic upbringing (possibly the whitest clown of them all) and her attraction to love and eroticism. We can be reasonably certain, too, that Zampano will not look upon the next waif he picks up as an Auguste to be scorned and abused.

4
Characters and Identity

Fellini's films, from *La strada* to *Juliet of the Spirits*, are about people who are dissatisfied with their lives, although none of them knows exactly why. They search for an antidote to the discontent they feel, even though they cannot place its cause. Gelsomina comes closest to knowing what it is that she seeks—a purpose—and she vaguely comprehends that she might find it if she meant something to Zampano. Cabiria only knows that she wants her life to "change," a desire which repeatedly gets her involved with unscrupulous men. Other characters are not even aware that it is emptiness they feel. Guido simply wants to cure his exhaustion and Marcello to relieve his boredom. Augusto is confident that he will feel fine as soon as he becomes a top confidence artist and Giulietta is bewildered that her ideal marriage is not the last word in bliss. Whether or not they admit it to themselves, these people are alone—some because of their background, some because of their own selfishness, and some because they have never had the opportunity to reach other people. Fellini's films deal with the need human beings have for each other and the personal and social factors which frustrate its fulfilment.

The remnants of childhood experience and a predilection for the absolutes of early life over the uncertainties of adulthood are integral to the make-up of most of Fellini's major characters. Fellini sees himself and his characters as trying to resolve a developmental conflict of sorts. They need to move from a secure, almost womblike, universe that is centred around themselves, to one in which the importance of other people is recognised. This is Fellini's private, intuitive, non-analytical scheme of psycho-development. It is concerned with the way a person feels rather than with any aberrations of behaviour and a "subconscious" has no valid role in his scheme. (The weakest moment of *Juliet of the Spirits* is when Giulietta finds the secret door to her soul and frees herself from her childhood emotional trauma—a meaningless and evasive solution to her real problem.)

Checco, the Cavallis and the *vitelloni* have never progressed beyond Fellini's initial stage of development. They are perennial children. The *vitelloni*, in particular, have all the earmarks of a gang of young boys. They

101

Adults as children: as long as he is not challenged, Checco in VARIETY LIGHTS basks in self-satisfaction.

are remarkably agile at avoiding responsibility. Fausto packs his bags as soon as he learns that Sandra is pregnant, and when he unexpectedly finds himself among the employed, he sniffs the sleeve of his workcoat, puzzled by this garment that has suddenly confined him. His readiness to seize upon every opportunity for a new flirtation, without regard for its probable consequences to his marriage, confirms that he has never accepted the obligations that go with taking a wife. He even feels a youngster's immunity to punishment and sleeps peacefully with Sandra and the baby after receiving a transient fright from his strap-wielding father. Alberto insults the roadside workers, never dreaming that they will soon have a chance to retaliate. The escapade that results is the sort of thing one might expect from a gang of reckless juveniles. Moraldo goes along with whatever Fausto wants to do, even when he senses that it is wrong. All the characters of the early films respond immaturely to adversity: Fausto lies, Checco and Alberto pout, Ivan cries and Wanda overdramatises.

Each of these people lives within a closed cycle. At the end of their respective films, everything is essentially as it was at the beginning. Checco's misfortunes start when he tries to seduce a pretty girl on the train. When we last see him he is in exactly the same situation and on the verge of making an identical mistake. In *The White Sheik*, Wanda emerges from her encounter with the *fumetti* unit with her schoolgirl notions intact.

"*You* are my White Sheik," she tells Ivan, indicating that she has merely exchanged one impossible hero for another. Neither Checco, Wanda nor Ivan have learned a thing from their experiences. When Moraldo leaves home in *I vitelloni*, he leaves behind a town which will remain as it is for generations to come. Fausto will continue to chase women, Alberto will keep clowning and Leopoldo will write more worthless plays. Eventually they will all become like Fausto's father, settling down to raise their own *vitelloni*. Only Moraldo has broken free of the cycle. He has, for whatever reason, begun to experience the restlessness that bothers subsequent Fellini characters. He can never again be satisfied with the childlike status of his cronies.

Fellini does not rule out the possibility that people can be content in a kind of infantile state. Checco is much better off with his third-class vaude-villians than he would be with a more prestigious troupe, and Moraldo's friends will probably never be really unhappy with their lot. Even Ivan Cavalli will calm down when he returns to his own element. They are all easily satisfied by the achievement of their most immediate and self-grati-fying goals. Checco and Cavalli are happy as long as others seem to con-firm their senses of self-importance. Checco's infatuation with Liliana starts as a power play, an attempt to use his position in a casting couch seduction. He becomes pathetically lovesick only when his dominance over her is threatened, first by Renzo and then by Anselmo. He is most despondent

Adults as children: the vitelloni *are perennial adolescents. From I VITELLONI. Riccardo (Riccardo Fellini) at left, then Alberto and Leopoldo.*

when he has clearly lost control of his protege. In the same way, Cavalli is the model of authoritarianism until his bride and the rest of the world begin to behave in ways which ignore the meticulous plans he has made for them. It would never occur to either man that his life is not absolutely complete and correct in itself. This is exactly the attitude of the *vitelloni*, each of whom has unqualified confidence in his own judgement and ability. Fausto, for instance, always feels that someone else is to blame for his problems: it was Giulia who made a pass at him, his employer deserved to be robbed, his domestic difficulties could only be due to misunderstandings on the part of Sandra and her father. Alberto protests his sister's affair with a married man because he is afraid his friends will make fun of him. Leopoldo revels in his image as an artist. As long as his companions accept him as a playwright, he feels no need to question the worth of what he pens.

These people are childlike, provincial and entrenched in self-satisfaction. As such, they embody the origins of the protagonists in Fellini's later films. These country people are Guido and Marcello before they sensed that something was missing in their lives. Smugness provides the heroes of Fellini's first movies with a protective shelter against bothersome philosophical questions regarding their relationships to those around them and to the world as a whole. It is part of a comfortable, juvenile stage of develop-

Adults as children: Checco's relationship with Milena is almost that of a mother and son in VARIETY LIGHTS.

Adults as children: Fausto in I VITELLONI has never accepted the responsibility of marriage. His continual flirtations (above) repeatedly cause him remorse (below).

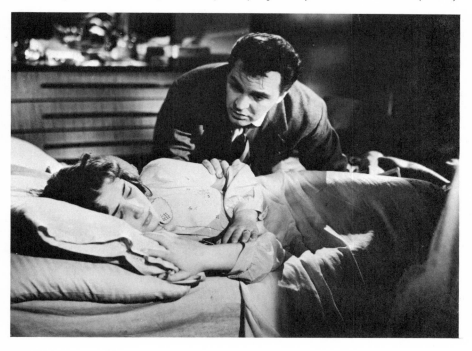

ment—so comfortable that men like Guido and Marcello often long to return to it. But they, like Moraldo and like Fellini himself, have felt a requirement for meaningful contact with other people and are beyond the point where a regression to easier days can give them contentment.

In the characters of Fellini's first films we can discern some of the forces of childhood that play such an important role in the emotional make-up of his later protagonists. The structure of the family is among the strongest of these forces. Most of the *vitelloni* live at home with their parents. Alberto nearly collapses into his mother's arms when his sister leaves with the married man. His half-drunken sobbing is meant to be in sympathy with his mother's grief, but when he starts to have second thoughts about his hasty promise to find a job, we see that it is he who is seeking consolation. (There is a similarly motivated outburst from Il Patacca in *Amarcord* when Miranda, his sister and mealticket, dies.) Fausto, despite his age, is dominated by his father who forces him to wed the pregnant Sandra and later beats him. His father-in-law exercises equivalent authority when he makes him take the job at the religious articles store. Ivan Cavalli begins his own marriage by trying to play the bossy, strong willed man-of-the-house. In coming to Rome he is intent upon pleasing his uncle, whom he takes to be an important man. He is nervous about filing a missing person report for fear of embarrassing his relatives, and becomes absolutely horrified when the police interrogator asks for his father's name. "Nobody must find out," he pleads, "My father's a councilman and my uncle is an important Vatican official." The last straw for Milena, in *Variety Lights*, comes when Checco, on the way back from Renzo's, doesn't stop to help her father when he stumbles and falls. The next sequence takes place in Rome and Checco is with Liliana. But when Checco falls upon hard times and is abandoned by his stage struck discovery, he turns first to Milena for help. It is very nearly the act of a wayward son returning to his mother for aid and forgiveness. Ultimately he embarks upon another tour with his original troupe. Despite the petty bickering and jealousies, there is a kind of family spirit among the ensemble. Checco has a well-defined place within it and he can count upon loyalty and "variety spirit" to prevail even after moments of intense strain. For Checco, as for Ivan, Fausto and Alberto, it is important to have a close, familiar group on which to fall back. In the end it is always easier to answer to one's own family than to a hostile, outside world. It is significant that Moraldo's first step in seeking a broader, more satisfying life is to break free from his family and from the group of *vitelloni*—which is a kind of family in itself. We should also note that the event which throws Gelsomina's serene existence into chaos is separation from her mother and sisters.

The views of Rimini afforded by *Roma* and *Amarcord* reinforce the impressions about the comfort and tenacity of family life garnered from *Variety Lights*, *The White Sheik* and *I vitelloni*. In *Amarcord*, Titta's family is a refuge of moral strength in a town that is innundated with Fascism and unattainable dreams. His father, tortured by the Fascists over

the incident of the gramophone, is the only point of political resistance in
the entire place. The death of the mother is a turning point for the film,
an irretrievable loss which leads into the final failure of illusion—Gradisca's
wedding to a local policeman. The bereavement occurs at the height of
the film's winter. In *Roma*, the *pensione* and *trattoria* are among Fellini's
most pleasant memories of the city. Despite their size, both institutions
have the atmosphere of a family affair. What could be more natural than
for the young Fellini, freshly arrived from the only home he has known, to
seek a replacement family? There are striking similarities between the
family quarters in *Amarcord* and the *pensione* in *Roma*. And the moment
in *Roma* when the sunburned man curls up beside his massive mother—
although it is offered in a comic vein—has the same ring as the scene between Alberto and his mother in *I vitelloni* and the visit to the hospital
in *Amarcord*. The ties that one has to one's family are ready made, ex-
tremely emotional and simple to maintain. Parents give their children a
great deal and make few demands in return. When they do ask for something, compliance is rarely difficult.

The concept of honour goes hand-in-hand with reverence for the family.
Matters of honour are among the few situations in which parents are likely
to require sacrifices from their offspring. Almost all the pressure experienced
by Fausto involves the preservation of respectability. "Sandra's father is
an honourable man like me," his father shouts at him while insisting that
he marry the pregnant girlfriend. Later, when Fausto loses his job, he is
berated as much for damaging the honour of his father-in-law as for making
a pass at Giulia or stealing the statue. Alberto's stated objection to his
sister's affair is that it will disgrace him, although he is also worried about
the loss of her ready monetary handouts. Ivan Cavalli takes the principle
of honour to the most absurd extreme of all. Throughout his ordeal he
never feels that he has lost someone he loves. His only concern is to save
face. The priority he gives to honour is no less ridiculous than Wanda's
romantic fantasies. This point becomes obvious when Fellini merges the
two tendencies—honour and romance—during Wanda's suicide attempt. The
sequence is full of romantic gestures that go haywire—gags that ridicule
the idea of taking such drastic action for honour. Her passionate suicide
note—delivered via the unorthodox medium of the telephone—sounds idi-
otic when it is read back. Both the style (Wanda pinches her nostrils shut)
and outcome of the attempt emphasise its foolishness, as do the shots of
angelic statues that precede her jump. It is easy to understand how the
substitution of honour for love and ethical behaviour in childhood might
lead to the moral indolence and selfishness that trouble Guido and Marcello.

Mysticism is another quality of childhood that stays with Fellini's characters into adult life. The children in his films have an inherent affinity
for occultism. They see anything that they do not understand, or anything
that is out of the ordinary, in supernatural terms. This includes such diverse phenomena as nature, sex, people with bizarre appearances or behaviour and spectacle of all sorts, from movies to Fascist demonstrations.

The family: in AMARCORD, Titta's family is the most important part of his life. At home, his mother (Pupella Maggio) is often hyper-excitable.

Furthermore, children like repetitive, ritualised chants and movements: The little boy in the *pensione* in *Roma* who protrudes his tongue again and again, the spontaneous hand clapping and jumping up and down during Saraghina's rhumba in *8½* and the circular dance of the children at the end of *La strada* are not far removed from the "Asa Nisi Masa" gestures in *8½* or the way the youngsters in *La strada* clap and mark time as they encircle Gelsomina and Oswaldo. Fellini picks up the rhythm of these movements and makes it the rhythm of the sequence in which they occur. In *8½*, this rhythm lays stress on the magical properties of a secure childhood where everything one needs, including love, is instantly provided. In *La strada*, it stresses Gelsomina's bond with the children on one hand, and with Oswaldo on the other.

The church both encourages and capitalises upon the child's propensity for mysticism. Fellini, like so many of his characters, has tried to come to terms with his Catholic education. But the church labels as "divine" values which are reactionary, at least in view of the character's struggle to escape his self-centred origins. Family, honour and an abiding concern for one's own soul all receive the heavenly seal of approval. Everything that falls outside this field is marked as evil and carries the threat of damnation and supernatural torture. The priests use their mythology to frighten the child

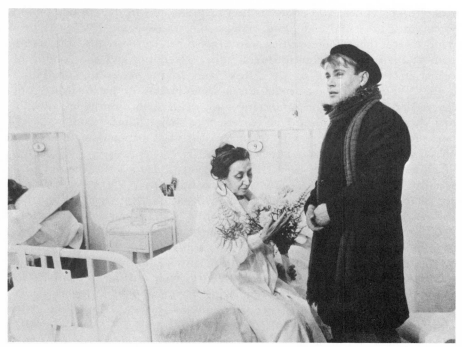

The family, in AMARCORD, Titta's closeness to his mother is emphasised in the visit to the hospital just before her death.

into observing their standards. "Don't you know that Saraghina is the devil?" the father superior asks young Guido. "St. Luigi cries when you masturbate," Don Balosa tells Titta in *Amarcord*, while pointing to a statue of the saint. With lessons like these behind him, it is little wonder that Marcello is irresistibly attracted to Sylvia when he accompanies her to the top of St. Peter's. This earthy woman, whom Marcello later calls a "goddess," combines the ethereal and the forbidden as she cavorts in a quasi-clerical outfit high above the Vatican. Similarly Giulietta seems both to trust and to fear Lynx-eyes, the detective, when he first appears dressed· as a priest. His clothing strikes a responsive chord in her, indicating that he is omniscient and certain to be in the right as an arbiter of marital problems. Giulietta has been more profoundly touched by religious mysticism than any other Fellini character. Therefore, it is quite reasonable that she should envision death as a little girl who is damned because she committed suicide for love. Fellini's depiction of the devil as an evil little girl in *Toby Dammit* may have a similar origin.

Most of Fellini's leading characters bear the marks of having grown up in Romagna under the influence of their families and the church. Priests have controlled a good portion of their educations and reality has seldom been harsh enough to interfere with their fantasies. They come from a society which is nearly as closed as that of the monks in the episode Fellini wrote for *Paisa*. And like those monks, the townspeople link their own identities to their communities. (In *Amarcord*, for example, the entire town shares in the celebration of Gradisca's wedding and the coming of spring, in the cheering of the "Rex" and in the mourning of Titta's mother.) This still leaves room for a wide variety of personalities, but Checco and Ivan Cavalli, for instance, are reduced to nothingness outside their own groups. Ivan and Checco return to their "homes" and the *vitelloni*, except Moraldo, never leave theirs. But what happens to those who pursue their identities in a larger universe?

Gelsomina's adventures reflect the problems of many other Fellini protagonists. When we first see her, she is walking near the sea carrying a bundle of sticks on her back. She is shown only in long shot or from behind, so her face is not clearly seen. In this barren, lonely introduction, her only visible link to the rest of the world is the sea. By any standard, she is quite nondescript. Even among her family she has no distinguishing features and is simply one of many children. In selling her daughter away, Gelsomina's mother doesn't mention the girl's own attributes, but tries to interest Zampano in the deal by comparing her to an older sister, Rosa. So in departing with her new master, Gelsomina is leaving behind the only identity she has ever known, that of her family. As she goes, Gelsomina's younger sisters run after her, waving goodbye. Zampano's motorcycle car gathers speed and she sees the children recede into the distance, as in the shots of Moraldo's friends and relatives as his train leaves town. Both Gelsomina and Moraldo are abandoning their childhood indentities and will soon have to define themselves with respect to new people in a less sheltered world.

Gelsomina's first response to this problem is to attempt to rework herself into Zampano's image. She tries hard to imitate him, blowing the trumpet as he does and taking his direction for the hunter and duck routine. Later, at supper, she follows his lead in chewing on a toothpick. She is proud to be associated with Zampano and beams approvingly even while he tries to seduce another woman. It is important to Gelsomina that she act in a manner which will please him since he has replaced her mother and sisters as her point of self-reference.

In principle, Gelsomina's new attitude suits Zampano well. He wants a servant—somebody who will adapt to him without making reciprocal demands. His needs and character are basic and he has little tolerance for Gelsomina's non-pragmatic side. When she plants the tomatoes, he is astounded that anyone would cultivate vegetables that they will not be able to eat. He is contemptuous of her simple-mindedness and of the mysticism that goes into the charm she recites besides the campfire. He has no doubts as to who he is and expects everyone else to conform to his sensible way of seeing things. When Gelsomina asks where he is from, he replies, "My parents." When she repeats the query, he says, "My father's house." His tone is sarcastic as if the answers were obvious from the start. He has never felt any compulsion to look beyond himself.

Gelsomina feels that her alliance with Zampano is more than a simple master-servant relationship. From the night Zampano forces her to sleep with him, she regards him as her husband. That is the first time he asks her name, and after his inattentiveness to her, the question has more or less the force of a marriage proposal. Following her reluctant honeymoon, she accepts Zampano as the focus of her life and is particularly pleased when, as a matter of convenience in the restaurant, he refers to her as his wife. Just prior to the Oswaldo sequence a man brings Gelsomina a drink while she is performing for the children. She takes a sip from the glass and carries the rest to Zampano. She does this out of a genuine wish to share things with him and not because it is an obligation of her servitude.

During the course of her short life with Zampano, Gelsomina has several opportunities to desert him for groups which would accept her as part of a family. She ponders the circus owner's offer to take her into his troupe, but declines after Il Matto strengthens her resolve to stay with Zampano and seek a purpose for her life. The nuns at the convent take a strong liking to her, and after Zampano's attempt to pilfer the silver heart, one might expect Gelsomina to stay with her hostesses rather than accompany a conscienceless thief. But she has been affected by the words of one of the nuns: "We don't get attached to worldly things," the sister says, "You follow your husband and I follow mine." With this charge, Gelsomina's bond with Zampano is given a religious dimension—one that demands an unshakable faith in Il Matto's words and in her own worth. Even when she is near death, she refuses to join the kindly people who try to nurse her back to health. Her mind has been opened to questions that never disturbed her while she was at home—questions that cannot be answered by a return to her original family or by substituting a religious, professional or foster family for it. When Zampano abandons her, she loses the identity she has been building around him and, thus, ceases to exist.

Gelsomina's attitude toward her "marriage" is similar to that of the traditional Italian Catholic. (Gelsomina, of course, has no dogmatic religious awareness whatever. Her reactions are conditioned by Fellini's background.) Her union is consummated by the sex act and, once established, cannot be dissolved. Gelsomina gives herself over fully to Zampano and accepts the principle that self-realisation can only come from her being of use to him. When Zampano falls to his knees on the beach at the end of the film the doctrine appears to have been vindicated, as if it were part of some divine plan. Gelsomina has served a purpose: she has changed Zampano and made him aware of a requirement for other people in his life. It is a beautiful moment, certainly, and its power briefly draws our attention away from Gelsomina's personal tragedy. It may well be that the girl remains in contact with her husband through the continuums of nature and humanity. But in terms of her immediate needs—which are the most important to Fellini—her experience with Zampano is a total, and fatal, loss. Instead of searching for herself through or with Zampano, Gelsomina lets

In LA STRADA, Gelsomina is pleased to be part of Zampano's act and life.

herself be sacrificed for his sake. She makes her sense of self so dependent upon him that, finally, not a trace of her life remains except in Zampano. The emotionally ambiguous ending of *La strada* is a turning point, a new beginning, for Zampano; but it is a eulogy for Gelsomina. Its sadness is rooted in its sense of loss—not just Zampano's loss of Gelsomina, but Gelsomina's loss of life.

Gelsomina runs away from Zampano only once, but that adventure, and the events that precipitate it, point up the fear of loneliness that makes her cling to her husband with such determination. Early in the film, Gelsomina becomes conscious of the absence of love and companionship in her life, but her travels with Zampano do not correct the deficiency. When Zampano goes off with the redhead he meets in the restaurant, Gelsomina spends a desolate, frustrating night by herself. Then, on the day she leaves Zampano, she is involved in an accident which intensifies her pangs of loneliness. The couple set up a performance of their act at a big, rowdy wedding feast on a farm, but they remain clearly on the periphery of the general air of fun and joyfulness. Then some children take Gelsomina into a house where she is confronted with a peculiar looking, mute, atrophic child whose view is limited to the confines of his shut-in room. "That's Oswaldo," the children tell Gelsomina, "They never show him to anyone." At the children's urging, Gelsomina tries to make the bedridden creature laugh. But, suddenly, she stops, moves closer, and stares at him—not with fear or pity, but curiosity. There is an abrupt clearing of the mysticism with which the children have veiled the little boy and Gelsomina sees a pathetic, unhappy, totally isolated being. It is as though she were looking at herself in a mirror for the first time.

It takes a while for the full impact of the encounter with Oswaldo to filter through to Gelsomina. In her conversations with Zampano she mentions the meeting only in passing, but she has been affected implicitly by the sight of the secluded and underdeveloped cripple. That night, she tries to bring Zampano closer to her by recalling one of their better times together. ("Remember how good it was that day with the rain on the window?") and asking him to teach her to play the trumpet. Zampano, however, is preoccupied with a suit he is trying on and ignores her talk. Suddenly, influenced no doubt by the revelation of the afternoon, Gelsomina feels horribly alone and defeated. She walks to the wall and stands by herself for a minute. Then, in a paroxysm of anger, she hurls herself into a ditch. Zampano's only reaction is to ask if she intends to stay there all night. When she insists that she will, Zampano shrugs his shoulders and goes to sleep, leaving her in the throes of the worst loneliness and frustration she has ever known. Exasperated by his unconcern, Gelsomina decides to sneak away, vituperating Zampano as she goes. "I'm fed up," she complains to her sleeping husband, "I like the work. I like being an artiste. It's you I don't like." Then she confesses the real reason for her departure. "It's no use," she mutters, "he doesn't care about me." Her fear of being completely on her own is so great that she momentarily considers going home. But she is sidetracked by the religious festival and ends up in an empty square on a cold, windy night. When Zampano pulls up alongside her and barks at her to "get in," she makes only a weak display of protest before allowing herself to be forced into his vehicle. Although the quality of their relationship is far from satisfactory, at least she is not totally alone when she is with Zampano. It is better to stay with the brute and hope that he will change than to risk absolute solitude. What begins as a childish rebellion ends with Gelsomina recognising her own desperation.

Gelsomina's apprehension of not having anybody who cares about her is inseparable from her feeling of being of no use to anyone. So she is delighted when Il Matto reverses her perspective on this predicament. "If you don't stay with him," he asks, "who will?" His words, despite their mocking tone, give her a bit of self-esteem and a vague sense of superiority. She is rather taken with the image of power and importance they suggest, and boldly promises to do away with Zampano in a number of violent ways. But, for the time being, she announces, she will stay with him because, "If I don't, who will?"

If we get the impression that Il Matto has a healthy influence on Gelsomina, it is because he makes her feel that she has something of value to offer Zampano, and the ability to withdraw it of her own volition. The "madman's" lecture comes at a critical moment for her—Zampano is in jail and she has tentatively turned down the offer to travel with the circus.

She wants to wait for Zampano, but is unsure of herself. Only a few hours remain in which she can change her mind. As an adviser, perhaps the best thing Il Matto can do for Gelsomina is to point her attitude in a positive direction. But even if he makes her see things under a new light, he cannot alter the facts of her situation. He can only provide her with an article of faith which will furnish momentary consolation. However, when she takes to the road with Zampano again, this joy will disintegrate. As a purely religious figure, Il Matto has the same shortcomings as many priests in Fellini's films. The only comfort he can offer for the moment is his assurance that everything that troubles Gelsomina today fits into a greater, more meaningful scheme. But Gelsomina is not spared any misery by the transformation effected in Zampano after her death. (It is significant in this respect that the fulfilment of Gelsomina's purpose could only have happened after her death. If Zampano had found her before she died, they would, at best, have resumed their life together in the same unsatisfactory way as before Il Matto's murder.)

Il Matto's importance to Gelsomina, however, extends beyond his symbolic role as a heavenly advocate. At their first meeting Gelsomina stares at him in much the same way that she stared at Oswaldo. But instead of receiving a blank expression in return, Il Matto looks back at her with sympathy and understanding. Developmentally, Gelsomina is somewhere between Oswaldo and Il Matto. All three are lonely, mystical, and present a peculiar physical appearance. Oswaldo, however, has never had the chance to face the world and develop whereas Il Matto is well travelled and has learned to live with his loneliness. He protects himself with cynicism and a calculated madness that covers up his basic unhappiness without alleviating it. He instinctively attacks and harasses Zampano because the strongman is his natural enemy. Men like Zampano, who exploit and discard anyone who tries to get close to them, are responsible for the suffering of people like Gelsomina and Il Matto. Il Matto is Gelsomina's spiritual brother.

It may be that Gelsomina does not truly recognise her kinship with Il Matto until the moment of his death. After his murder her despondency is far deeper than simple grief for another person. Predicting his own death, Il Matto told her, "I will die someday and nobody will care." Her shocked response was to ask, "Not even your mother?" The realisation of Il Matto's prophecy brings out the identical nature of Gelsomina's own situation: her mother sold her immediately after learning that Rosa, another daughter, had died while on the road with Zampano. If Il Matto cannot survive, what chance can there be for her. She loses all hope for relief from her agonising loneliness.

Gelsomina's efforts to build a rapport with Zampano are hampered by her inability to make him understand her. Their relationship is an instance of the general problem of communication which vexes many of Fellini's characters as they strive to establish a personal equilibrium with others. From the very beginning, there is a total absence of effective communica-

In LA STRADA, Gelsomina proudly watches her "husband" in the restaurant.

tion between Gelsomina and Zampano. Most of the fault lies with Zampano, who is too wrapped up in himself to pay heed to what Gelsomina needs to tell him or to pick up on the emotional signals she sends him. That night in the farmyard, before she runs away from him, she wants to talk about the time they have spent with each other while he only wants to admire his newly acquired clothing. He would prefer that she simply not bother him and continually resists her attempts to draw him into conversation. When he tires of coarse evasions, as in the "where are you from?" exchange in the restaurant, he flatly tells her to shut up. That is his reaction when she asks him whether he "sleeps with all women" and when she questions him about his dispute with Il Matto. On the rare occasions when Zampano listens to her, he interprets her words to suit his own ideas. Once Gelsomina tells him that her home now seems to be with him. He misses the meaning of the statement entirely, agreeing that "with me you eat regularly." The same night, at the convent, Gelsomina seeks some small assurances of affection from him, only to be dismissed as a nuisance. Like his professional repertoire, Zampano's vocabulary is limited, covering only food, money and physical pleasure. His mistreatment of Gelsomina is thoughtless, not malicious. He can't give love because he doesn't understand it.

Gelsomina, in contrast to Zampano, is forever trying to express herself. Once she is freed from the isolation of her home life, she feels an overwhelming impulse to make contact with the man who has charge of her. At first, she uses the direct techniques of a child to provoke reactions from

In LA STRADA, Il Matto, Zampano's natural enemy, teases his adversary during the strongman's act.

Zampano. She makes faces, mimes, asks naively pointed questions, cries, and sulks. If her antics around the campfire and in the restaurant were not so honestly motivated, they would be little more than risible. But as Gelsomina grows in self-awareness and comes closer to finding an identity, she gains in her ability to communicate. After she has spent time with Il Matto, the girl begins to speak more coherently and maturely. Il Matto is the only person who addresses her with any degree of seriousness, and in doing so he helps her broaden her own communicative skills. He uses words and persuasion to give her new ideas—ideas which she will use in her subsequent bids to start a dialogue with Zampano. She speaks of belonging with Zampano, of having a purpose; she asks why he keeps her ("I can't cook, I'm not pretty," she says, recanting Il Matto's taunts) and whether he'd care if she died. When Il Matto, the source of her ideas, is killed, her evolving mastery of language breaks down rapidly. "He is sick," she babbles, "you killed him. It's pleasant here. He told me to stay with you. We need more wood." When Zampano, the object of the ideas, abandons her, she no longer has any need to talk. Later, when she is found by a concerned family, she has become completely mute.

Gelsomina never finds the identity she desires, but by owning up to her loneliness she does attain a certain degree of self-knowledge. Although Fellini, in his films, is still grappling with the problem of how to find one's place in the world, he seems to be convinced that the initial step must be a frank admission that one cannot amount to anything without others. Gelsomina becomes conscious of the void around her on the night she runs away. That is the first time she hums her song—a sad, simple, vibrant melody which begs for a consoling response from another musician. Later, when Il Matto plays the tune on his violin, it helps her recognise her propinquity to him. Gelsomina keeps playing the song even when she gives up speaking. It is the expression of her unremitting loneliness, the only self-certainty she has. After she passes away, the song lingers on to make Zampano aware of *his* loneliness and thus start him on the road of redemption.

There is a bit of Gelsomina inside the protagonists of all of Fellini's post *La strada* features, but the most direct descendants of the waif are the two other Masina characters, Cabiria and Giulietta. Each of them, like Gelsomina, has her complacency destroyed unexpectedly, forcing her to try to define a new role for herself or face insufferable loneliness. Both women are shackled in some way to the beliefs and aspirations of childhood and both are troubled by ineffective communication. Neither of them, however, is simply a pale version of Gelsomina. Through Cabiria and Giulietta, Fellini examines facets of the loneliness problem that are beyond the scope of Gelsomina's life. *Nights of Cabiria* and *Juliet of the Spirits* look at both the rudimentary problems between people and the way certain institutions complicate these problems. But beneath the modernity and sophistication of the films' heroines, we still have, in essence, Gelsomina.

Cabiria is every bit as lonely as Gelsomina, but she refuses to admit it,

In LA STRADA, Gelsomina's second meeting with Il Matto occurs in a mystical setting. The tent flaps in a magical wind as Il Matto plays Gelsomina's song.

NIGHTS OF CABIRIA: Cabiria's bravado leads her to the swank Via Veneto.

staunchly maintaining that she is self-sufficient. Her much repeated boast, "I have everything I need," is really a denial, or at least an evasion, of her need for other people. She refutes, as if by reflex, any inference that she might require help from anyone. When she is saved from drowning at the beginning of the film, she immediately depreciates her debt to her rescuers by belittling them. "All right," she yells, "so you saved me. I'm going home." It takes her a long time to admit that Giorgio tried to drown her for her money. But when this reality eventually sinks in, she is morose only for a moment, cuddling a chicken as though it were her only friend in the world. Then, quickly turning her thoughts from her unhappiness to her wounded pride, she throws the chicken into the air and chides herself angrily for having been such a fool. She runs into the house, gathers Giorgio's belongings and tosses them into the fire. Afterwards, in exasperation, she gestures sharply at nobody in particular. Her fierce sense of pride and independence are really affectations which she uses to distract herself from her loneliness.

Cabiria's self-assertive manner is mostly bluff. She has been out and around long enough to be suspicious of things that seem too perfect or too providential. Still, distrust does not come naturally to her, so she must constantly work at keeping up this appearance of sophistication and emotional detachment. Unfortunately, Cabiria usually is able to convince no one but herself that she possesses these qualities—and she convinces herself so well that she develops a heady self-confidence, especially in situations which appeal to her curiosity or touch upon her basic interests. Then her scepticism breaks down and she becomes most vulnerable to the people who want to use or deceive her. She falls for Giorgio because he seems to offer her the love for which she yearns. She remains on her guard with Oscar until she has put him to the test by threatening to leave him. When, as she hoped, he proposes marriage, Cabiria feels that she has outsmarted him and leaves herself open to the forthcoming disaster. In fact, the tragic chain of events with Oscar begins when Cabiria boasts of her money and independence to the hypnotist, effectively inviting exposure.

The adventure with the actor demonstrates, under relatively benign circumstances, the way Cabiria's bluffing operates and the fragility of that *facade*. The episode begins with a show of bravado. Incensed at a pimp's suggestion that she could benefit from his services, Cabiria tells him to drop her off at Via Veneto. Her demand is a gesture of defiance towards the procurer. He laughs at her, and with good reason: nobody could be less at home among the street's swank night-clubs and their clientèle than Cabiria. But once she alights from the car, she feels that she must follow through on her boast. So she puffs herself up and tries to imitate the gait of two high-class streetwalkers who are parading back and forth on the sidewalk. The result is amusing both for its unnaturalness and its put-on disdainfulness.

Later that night, when the actor picks her up, Cabiria appears not to be impressed by him. "What is this?" she complains, refering to the curt way he commands her to get in and out of his car. But at the night-club, he is her proof of importance. Once she is safely inside ("I'm with him," she tells the doorman, knowing that she could not gain admittance otherwise), she actually begins to believe that her good fortune is her own doing and her confidence begins to grow. However, her vision of having cracked chic society is obviously a delusion. She is not quite sure of what to do with her umbrella at the checkroom, and she has difficulty navigating the slit in the curtain which separates the foyer and the cabaret. But as long as her escort is the centre of attention, she can sidetrack some of his glory to herself. Every woman in the establishment watches enviously as she dances with the actor and Cabiria basks in what she interprets as their high regard of her. When the prostitute is happiest, she breaks away from the movie star and launches into a wild, uninhibited dance. Cabiria's mambo is a spontaneous expression of herself which emerges automatically when she is at her most euphoric. Her gyrations bring looks of amused condescension from those around her, and if Cabiria were to notice and understand these expressions, she would be deeply hurt.

While Cabiria is in the actor's company, we view her boasts of success in the light of his indisputable personal and professional accomplishments. He is of high social status and, therefore, besieged by pretentious, artificial people who want favours or to be seen in his presence. He finds Cabiria's impetuousness and lack of guile refreshing in comparison to the brazenness of the people who are attracted by his celebrity. After Cabiria mildly scandalises this night-club crowd with her freewheeling dance, the actor's attitude toward her softens. Perhaps her behaviour makes him understand that, despite Cabiria's airs, she is not truly concerned with rising in the world or impressing people. Deep down, her dance says, she just wants to find a satisfying realisation and expression of herself.

The actor takes Cabiria to his villa which is a substantial piece of real estate, an end product of his achievements. His luxurious quarters are a physical extension of his presence, an effect which is so overpowering that Cabiria feels compelled to flaunt her own proof of identity. As usual, this consists of an itemisation of her property. She chatters on about owning a house with electricity, running water, bottled gas and even a thermometer. "Of course," she acknowledges, "it's nothing like this. But it's just right for me." Cabiria is self-conscious about the disparity between her dwelling and that of her host, but she is determined to go on faking it. She tries to persuade herself that she is relatively unimpressed by the exotic villa, just as she makes herself believe that she has seen and enjoyed one of the actor's movies. If she did not deceive herself this way, she would be defaulting on a challenge to her identity and admitting to a feeling of personal disorientation and insignificance. Her house gives her an address; it gives her shelter, comfort and a place to return to no matter what befalls her. It is the only tangible evidence of her existence and it provides her with an identity analogous to that given other Fellini characters by their families. Therefore, whenever Cabiria feels insecure, as in the music-hall, she talks about her house. The actor's elaborate accommodation dwarfs hers, so she is forced not only to tell about her property, but to defend its adequacy. In doing so, she is defending her own adequacy in the face of someone who is better established than she.

When we look at Cabiria's house objectively and compare it to the actor's, it is plain that her defence cannot hold up. The actor's house has been built and furnished in his own image. It is vast, glittering and showy—perfect for a matinee idol. It is adorned with an incongruous assortment of *objets d'art*, which seems appropriate for a man who loves to lie back and be wafted away by Beethoven's Fifth Symphony. Cabiria's house, on the other hand, is absolutely nondescript. It is square, strictly utilitarian and situated on a dismal tract of land. It bears no resemblance whatsoever to the lively creature who inhabits it. Cabiria's idiosyncratic behaviour and need for love tell us that she is somebody unique; her house, though, says that she is nobody special. Cabiria cannot find herself until she is free of the house and the attitude that it signifies. Her property is even a cause of her problems with men, drawing the attention of Giorgio and Oscar who want to relieve her of it. When her affair with Oscar irrevocably separates her from that property, her life must "change." At that point she has the same potential for development and encountering others that Moraldo and Gelsomina have when they leave their homes.

The variety hall episode suggests an association between Cabiria's regard for property and her childhood ideals. The sequence comes after the *débacle* at the shrine where the church treacherously uses the lives and

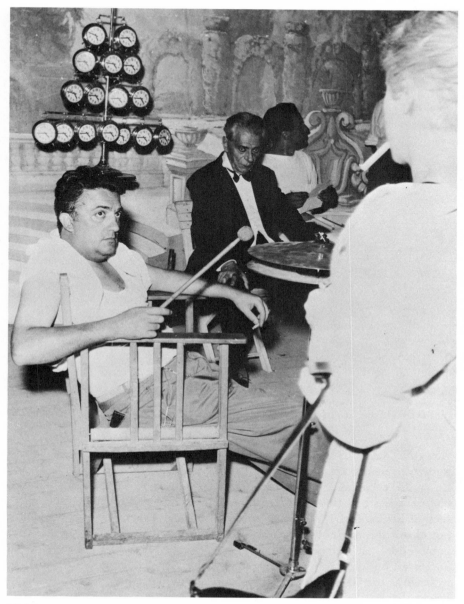

NIGHTS OF CABIRIA: Fellini, Giulietta Masina and Silvani discuss the hypnosis sequence between takes.

hopes of hundreds to fuel its own spectacle. The activities at the shrine have critically upset Cabiria's delicate equanimity, causing her to question the state of her life, in spite of her protective habit of self-deception. On stage, at the variety show, her confidence is shaken further by a man wearing plastic horns (a figure exactly opposite to the shrine's holy virgin) who

NIGHTS OF CABIRIA: Cabiria dances under the hypnotic spell of the magician (Silvani).

turns her carefully hidden fears into a source of diversion for a boorish audience. Before the jeering crowd Cabiria again insists that she has everything she needs and that she is not so foolish as to want to get married. She even lies and claims to live in a well-to-do-neighbourhood. But with a flick of his hand the hypnotist brushes aside her defiant veneer. He impels her to tell the truth—that she lives on the Ostia Road behind the gas company—and then he regresses her to adolescence. Behind Cabiria's *braggadoccio* we find a simple, radiant child—a shy girl with long black hair who is anxious to receive the affections of a suitor described by the magician. When she waltzes with her imaginary *fiancé*, we see how badly she needs a partner of flesh and blood. Suddenly, as though the trance were not strong enough to hold back the fears of the adult Cabiria, she starts to cry. "You're not trying to deceive me, are you?" she asks, half inquiring, half imploring. As an adult, the innocence of childhood is no longer accessible to Cabiria, although her requirement for security persists. She tries to fulfil this requirement by substituting affluence and independence for the love and contact with other people she really needs. Even her profession is based upon an exchange of pleasure for money. But just as the yellow dye she uses can only temporarily disguise her naturally dark hair, her status seeking cannot truly and permanently replace the needs she has felt since she was eighteen years old.

Cabiria and Gelsomina want essentially the same thing: the contentment of having a special place in the world. If just one person would recognise them as unique and important, even in a private sense, they would be enormously happy. At root, it is a matter of having outside confirmation of their individuality. Gelsomina hunts for a purpose that will be hers alone and believes that she will have it if she makes herself indispensable to Zampano. She oversteps, however, and eventually surrenders her entire being to him. A person who becomes a mere appendage of another loses her own identity. Cabiria, also, would like to find someone who would give her a special place in his life, but the Oscars and Giorgios she meets in her business are not likely candidates. In lieu of such a relationship, Cabiria tries to win recognition by acquiring marks of status. We see from her night at the actor's villa, though, that the kind of achievements that make the world take notice are far beyond her range.

In the last Masina film, *Juliet of the Spirits*, we find a woman who might be the materialisation of either Gelsomina's or Cabiria's dreams. Giulietta has a husband to whom she has given herself completely, and he has accepted by having her take his name. Gelsomina wanted the same thing from Zampano. And Giulietta has a house that, in most respects, rivals that of Cabiria's actor. Maids take care of her mundane chores and she has conveniences that are dramatic advancements over bottled gas and a thermometer. Giulietta even moves in a fashionable society that would probably regard Via Veneto as a tourist trap.

By the standards of her predecessors in *La strada* and *Nights of Cabiria*, Giulietta should be perfectly content. Yet, she has all the problems that disturbed Gelsomina and Cabiria. Giulietta's husband, Giorgio, does not always act like Zampano; he seems to treat her with consideration and discretion. But Giorgio cheats on his wife, not openly like Zampano, but surreptitiously, feeling that everything will be fine as long as he does not disrupt his formal relationship with her. Although Giorgio plays husband to Giulietta by the book, he acts as if she had no independent feelings or intelligence. He lies to her and never seems to acknowledge her distress over his calling a strange woman's name in his sleep or making covert phone calls to his mistress in the middle of the night. He just assumes that his wife will accept his facile denials and explanations of the incidents. Even during the awkward moments before he leaves with his girl-friend, he pretends that nothing is seriously amiss. In one shot Giorgio lies peacefully in bed, with his back to Giulietta and a black sleeping mask covering his eyes. This image implies that Giorgio is as non-communicative and closed off to his wife as Zampano was to his. The picture of Giorgio as a beast and threat to Giulietta is clearest during the scene on the terrace with Jose,

JULIET OF THE SPIRITS: above, despite their affluence, there is little communication between Giulietta (Giulietta Masina) and Giorgio (Mario Pisu); below, Giulietta looks very plain walking between her mother (Caterina Boratto) and her sister (Sylva Koscina).

the romantic Spaniard who is a business associate of Giorgio. Jose speaks admiringly of the bullfighter's internal rhythm, spontaneity, and purity of heart while Giulietta tries a pass using her red scarf as a cape. Giorgio stands in for the bull, making monstrous, snarling faces.

As for her beautiful beachside house, Giulietta is more its prisoner than its proprietress. Her maids, though properly polite, do not have a high regard for her and one of them even carries on flagrantly with a boy-friend during working hours. The house itself is decorated, for the most part, in white. The maids also wear white as they glide around the premises doing their work like efficient nurses in an antiseptic hospital. The house is comfortable but not warm, elaborate but not distinctive. Its grounds are meticulously manicured without a single blade of grass out of place. The estate's cold, sterile atmosphere offers even less excitement than Cabiria's field along the Ostia Road. This bleached, ordered world belongs to Giorgio and Giulietta has fit herself into it because she also belongs to him.

Her house and legitimate marriage aside, Giulietta is in precisely the same predicament as Cabiria and Gelsomina. The first few minutes of *La strada*, *Nights of Cabiria* and *Juliet of the Spirits* have one important similarity—the face of the main character is not shown until the action is well underway. This device has different implications for each of the films, but it also points out a consideration that is common to the trilogy. Whether they realise it or not, Gelsomina, Cabiria, and Giulietta all live in a state of veritable anonymity and each is indistinguishable from others of her class. Giulietta is a faceless fixture in her own home. When she dresses in white, as she so often does, she blends in with the building's fixtures. Walking back from the beach, plain, pale Giulietta might as well be invisible next to her eye-catchingly attired mother and sister. Her state of anonymity is explicitly described in the spirit message to Giulietta during the seance. "Who do you think you are?" the communicant from beyond demands. "You're no one to anybody. You don't count, you wretched thing."

Giulietta, however, is unlike Gelsomina or Cabiria in that her situation never causes her outright despair. Compared to Gelsomina's eagerness and Cabiria's aggressiveness, Giulietta is passive and resigned. Because she has grown up under the influence of the church, which frowns upon spiritual freedom and originality, she has never felt her own vitality. Before she can walk out her front gate into a rich new world of experience, she must shed the church-instilled inhibitions that have prevented her from discovering her true needs and potential.

The most directly troublesome of these church-laid snares is the Catholic ideal of marriage—the control and institutionalisation of love. On the way to Bhishma's reading, Giulietta pauses for a moment to watch a wedding party in another room. A priest is charging the groom to "Love your wife like yourself, because he who loves his wife loves himself. Love for better or for worse, for richer or for poorer, in health or in sickness." The party pleases her because it is a re-affirmation that love means marriage and that it is secure, permanent and inviolable. The celebration assuages the faintness she felt when the spirit told her she meant nothing to anyone. According to the church, it is the fact of her marriage and not its condition that makes her whole—a doctrine which makes her accept and rationalise her husband's disappointing conduct at any cost. She tells her sister that Giorgio never takes her anywhere, attributing his lack of attention to her as weariness. Someday, she says, only half convinced, she and Giorgio will take a vacation together. Although she is confused and unhappy at the signs of Giorgio's cheating, she would rather not be confronted first hand with irrefutable proof of his infidelity. She tries to turn back when Adele takes her to see Lynx-eyes, the detective, because if he demonstrates that her marriage has failed, the entire structure of her life will fall to pieces.

Giulietta might never have allowed herself to face the truth about Giorgio were it not for a series of events which impresses her with the dearth of pleasure in her "model" existence. The church, of course, makes no allowance for pleasure in marriage. Matrimony is a duty, a holy state, but not an arrangement for physical gratification. This policy is a typical instance of the church not meeting—and actually threatening—the needs of a Fellini character. Giulietta is receiving little sexual satisfaction from "poor, tired" Giorgio, so she suppresses her desire in order to avoid throwing her religious convictions into crisis. But wherever she turns, she encounters reminders of her muzzled passion. These often take the form of small incidents or comments—Jose's visit, the maid's boy-friend, the sculptress's affairs with her muscular, adonis models, and the doctor's prescription for every ill: "Have your husband make love to you more often." But none of these are as disconcerting as the afternoon with Bhishma or the visits with Suzy.

The seance at the house and the visions on the beach set the stage for Bhishma. At the seance, Giulietta precipitates a conflict between two opposing internal tendencies. The exciting message of "Love for everyone" is borne by Iris, an alluring female spirit, while Olaf, a base Turk, calls everyone a whore and tells Giulietta that no one loves her. By the sea, the next day, Giulietta closes her eyes and suddenly Iris appears, sitting on her swing over the water and smiling invitingly. The next apparition, though, is of a Turkish barge full of frightening figures that threaten death. While Giulietta is enticed by the hope for free and unlimited love promised by Iris, her upbringing has led her to regard such a thing as pagan and barbarous.

The androgynous medium, Bhishma, is a personification of Giulietta's confusion. The spiritualist serves as another battleground for Olaf and Iris, both of whom manifest themselves to Giulietta in the course of the "sitting." In her trance, Bhishma confuses love and whorishness and obscenely caresses her own shriveled body while ranting insanely about her beauty. Bhishma also tells Giulietta that her husband should be her god and she the priestess of his cult. "Your spirit . . ." she goes on, "must burn and smoke on the altar of your loving body." This prefigures the sculptress's comment that she wishes to chisel powerful, masculine gods who could make love to her. Such ideas are decidedly non-Catholic.

JULIETS OF THE SPIRITS: Suzy (Sandra Milo) becomes Giulietta's instructor in matters of eroticism.

Suzy makes her first appearance between the vision of Iris and the vision of the Turks, and combines features of both apparitions. She is played by the same actress as Iris (Sandra Milo) and she arrives at the beach on an Oriental barge. Suzy lives right next door to Giulietta, but in a completely separate world. On the outside, Suzy's house looks as if it were deserted. The lawn is overgrown with wild plants and flowers, leaves are everywhere and the *facade* is faded and cracking. The structure seems strange and mysterious at first glance, but inside a party is usually in progress.

Suzy handles her sensuality naturally and without the least taint of shamefulness. She keeps every imaginable facility and accessory for pleasure within easy reach. Men worship her and are happy to spend their lives in the erotic luxury of her mansion while they wait for her to turn her attention to them. The atmosphere is grotesque in its excessiveness, but it holds an irresistible appeal for Giulietta who knows neither pleasure nor adoration. In Suzy's company Giulietta is exposed, head on, to all of her conditioned reservations about sex. She sees pleasure taken as an end in itself and hears Suzy admire the sweaty, muscular, loinclothed body of one of her guests. She nearly joins in a game in which the participants try to recreate the feeling of a bordello and act out their basest sexual fantasies. As she leaves Suzy's tree-top sundeck, she watches two youths ascend to the platform in a basket. Their elevator takes them along the trunk of the tall, straight tree through the hole in the platform, which Suzy is straddling.

Like everything else associated with Suzy, the image is blatantly sexual.
Yet, in the lush verdure of the forest, it is not at all offensive. Suzy, as Iris's
voice suggests, is teaching Giulietta that the things she has been led to
regard as disgusting are, in fact, normal and enjoyable. She is helping
Giulietta to unlearn some of her religious indoctrination. Her position is
the reverse of Suzy's dream where Giulietta, as a nun in a Catholic school,
flunks her for walking like a prostitute.

Suzy convinces Giulietta of her need for passion in an additional way—
by introducing her to Arlette. Arlette is a pale, short-haired girl who usually
remains in bed in a coach-house which is isolated from the activities in the
villa proper. She has become withdrawn and insane in the wake of three
suicide attempts over unhappy love affairs. Arlette reminds Giulietta of
Laura, a childhood friend who drowned herself for love, and whom Giulietta strongly associates with the child martyr from the school play. Just as
Oswaldo points out how alone Gelsomina is, Arlette indicates what is happening to Giulietta. As Giorgio's wife, Giulietta is also alone and underdeveloped in terms of self. By tying herself so firmly to Giorgio, by living
only for him and their marriage, Giulietta has committed a kind of spiritual
suicide. She has defaulted on her individuality, deprived herself of her
human and womanly potential and, therefore, is alone and unfulfilled
despite her home, friends and husband. The analogies to suicide for love
and to martyrdom for Catholic principle suit Giulietta well.

*JULIET OF THE SPIRITS: the child Guilietta begins her ascent to heaven in
the school pageant.*

Giulietta adheres to the repressive ideology of the church because she has never outgrown her childhood mysticism, the medium used to introduce the ideas in the first place. As a little girl, the school pageant about the child martyr seemed to be far more than an exercise to her. In the part of the juvenile defender of the church, she believed she would actually be carried to heaven and see God. If she had completed the role, she might have been disillusioned to the point of abandoning her Catholic expectations. Instead, her journey on the flaming grill was interrupted by her furious grandfather who properly denounced the play as perverse, absurd and unhealthy. So Giulietta continued to await the promised revelation by following the precepts given down by the nuns and headmaster.

Giulietta's grandfather exerted a strong influence in shaping the woman's reserved, ascetic emotional life. His hatred of pedantry, his lustful temperament and his escapade with the sensual circus artiste kept him at constant odds with the fountains of authority in Giulietta's life—the church, the headmaster and her mother. The bishop even applied the ecclesiastical mythology against him, declaring that he was in league with the devil. Consequently, the little girl rejected her grandfather's example, including the way he acted honestly on his feelings. Giulietta remembers him as the family's embarrassment, but when her spirits gather at the end of the film he and his trapeze artist are the only beneficent souls in the lot. Once Giulietta has freed herself from the martyr's grill to which the church restrained her, the Grandfather apparition tells her, "you don't need me any more . . . you are full of life."

It is not until the very end of the film that Giulietta recognises that she must choose between remaining a slave to the Catholic absolutisms of her youth, or growing and meeting her own needs. At first the problem is disguised as a contest between Iris and Olaf, but soon it emerges as a practical dilemma. Giulietta, under the guidance of Suzy (who is an incarnation of Iris) finds herself increasingly attracted to the possibility of leaving Giorgio and all that he represents. But such a move has ominous, horrifying implications while she is still under the sway of the church's teachings. Objectively, proof of Giorgio's infidelity should be an incentive for her to wrench herself free of her well-learned expectations about marriage. But the church could not abide this course and would insist that she regard the collapse of her marriage as the failure of her life, rather than the failure of one of the Vatican's eternal institutions. Lynx-eyes, the detective dressed as a priest, is the church's enforcer in this matter. It was he who Giulietta hallucinated on the beach, dragging the barge full of death and Turks—the church's bugaboos—to shore. At his office he tries first, in a benevolent guise, to dissuade his customer from prying further into her life. "Are you sure you won't be sorry later? You'd better stop and reflect," he suggests, assuming the role of a clerical marriage counsellor. "In similar cases I always advise a trip with the husband. Consider now the sweetness of a marriage maintained until old age, the tenderness of resting two white heads on the same pillow," he continues, reciting the church cant that

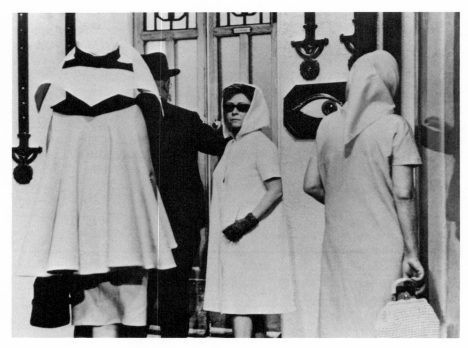

JULIET OF THE SPIRITS: Lynx-Eyes, the detective (Alberto Plebani), dresses like a priest and, to Giulietta, has the omnipotence of the church at his disposal.

Giulietta knows so well. If Giulietta carries the inquiry no further, then everything will go on as before. But because Adele will not allow her to baulk, and because her own desire to know is growing, her Catholic demons try another tactic. The fiery, stringent headmaster appears. "Woe to those who tolerate sin," he lectures, ". . . they become accomplices of the sinner and must burn with him . . . Claim your vengeance before the Lord." If Giulietta will not be bound by obedience, she can at least invoke the other mainstay of the church's ethic, justice.

Lynx-eyes himself leads the final assault of spirits which comes just after Giorgio has left with Gabriella, and Giulietta is on the verge of deciding what to do with herself. Dr. Miller, the psychotherapist, has explained Giulietta's difficulty to her, so Lynx-eyes needs to muster all the fears she has acquired since she was tiny in order to terrorise her back into submissiveness. The spectre of Laura even recommends death as Giulietta's least painful alternative. But Giulietta, in defiance of even her mother, finds the secret door to her past and unlashes her childhood from the martyr's grill. The spirits disperse and Giulietta, like a princess in a fairy tale, walks pleasantly into a brighter future.

While one must question the ease with which she frees herself, Giulietta, in the end, is unencumbered by her husband, her family, the church or the immature impressions and aspirations of childhood. She has gained a sense of herself as an adult. She is still aware of her need for love and recognition, and the friendly new spirits who chatter away in the last scene (perhaps they are premonitions of people she has yet to meet) are Fellini's way of indicating that she will find these things. But she will not repeat the mistakes of Gelsomina and Cabiria and turn herself over completely to a man, making her own worth and importance depend entirely upon him.

The male heroes of the post-*La strada* Fellini films have the same goals as the Masina characters. They are afraid of loneliness and need reassurance that they are not unnoticed in a teeming, impersonal world. But while they have Gelsomina's drive for purposefulness, they behave like Zampano in their relationships with others. Whereas Giulietta, Cabiria and Gelsomina are prepared to make any sacrifice to ensure that they are important to at least one person, Augusto, Marcello and Guido expect others to provide for their needs automatically and without compensation. They are unfair to their wives, mistresses and associates, not out of meanness, but because they are too preoccupied with themselves to realise that the people who fill crucial roles in their lives also have needs and expectations. They shut themselves off completely and then become distraught when nobody makes an effort to reach or help them. Under such circumstances, meaningful communication is impossible and one can never determine where one stands with others. The men in question have grandiose ambitions, but they cannot confidently announce themselves to the world at large until their definitive personal relationships are secure and in order. Otherwise, even they do not know who they are, and to be forced to proclaim oneself as nobody is, as Giulietta came to understand, tantamount to suicide. All three protagonists eventually face the prospect of such a suicide, but they avoid the dilemma for as long as they can through the expedient of lying.

For Augusto, lying is a way of life. As a swindler, his means of support depend upon falsehoods, but he, himself, is the victim of his most sustained deception. He has made himself believe that standing alone is a mark of distinction and that the key to satisfaction is competing with and defeating everybody else. Before leaving the night-club, Augusto complains about the calibre of his present accomplices. "I've been all over the world and I've conned everybody, because the world is full of fools," he says bitterly. "I could even sell ice to Eskimos. But now I have to work with these amateurs. I'm going back to working alone." His discourse reflects an inflated impression of his own prowess and a degradation of everybody else. His friendlessness, he implies, is the outcome of people's inability to reach his standard. Paradoxically, he puts the blame for his current lack of success upon his partners.

If Augusto regards his two colleagues as "amateurs," it is because each has an interest other than their con game. Roberto is a slick stylist who envisions himself as a pop singer—another Johnny Ray. The soaking of wealthy women and cheating of farmers are, in his mind, only diversions while he waits for his star to rise. Picasso has a wife and child and dreams of a happy, prosperous home. His recurring nightmare is that his wife, Iris,

IL BIDONE: Augusto considers his accomplices "amateurs". Roberto (Franco Fabrizi) and Picasso (Richard Basehart).

will become fed up with his erratic behaviour and return to her mother, taking their little girl with her. Considering their impulsiveness, conceit, irresponsibility and lack of intensity, both of these men bear a strong resemblance to the *vitelloni.*

There are many indications that Augusto once had much in common with his cohorts. He knows, presumably from personal experience, that Roberto's singing career is a pipe dream and that Picasso's *ego* and immaturity will prevent him from achieving a secure, productive marriage. Perhaps that is why Augusto's anger is laced with empathy when he tells Picasso that a family is poison in their line of work. At one time, Augusto had the same opportunity to have a home as Picasso, but, it is hinted, his ambition turned him away from the full, though unspectacular, contentment he might have found with his family. As a young man Augusto may not have been as susceptible to loneliness, but at the age of forty-eight he feels disgust over the years he has wasted in emptiness, and panic that he has so little time remaining. Not only does he lack the comfort and solace of friends, but his cravings for wealth and notoriety have gone wanting, as Rinaldo's party so painfully shows. Augusto has forsworn dependence upon other people, so swindling has become his entire sustenance and failure to get a break his sole excuse for his weariness.

Augusto's reaction to a chance meeting with his daughter, Patrizia, belies his mien of superior self-sufficiency. He immediately resolves to call her and invites her to spend Sunday afternoon with him. He even hints that he would like them to get together regularly after not seeing each other for so many years. In her presence he manages a kindness and concern that are at odds with his usual dour disposition. It is as if Patrizia had uncovered a side of Augusto that he had kept well hidden, even from himself. Besides bringing some freshness into his oppressive daily routine, she is a reminder of what he might have been had he acknowledged his need for other people when he had the opportunity. He is delighted when he sees a chance to do something for her—to regain her esteem—and offers to pay the 350,000 lire bond she must have to get a job.

His new pleasure and hope are destined to be short lived, however. The promise to raise the money excites Patrizia, but then so does the worthless swindlers' wristwatch Augusto gives her. The new relationship, like the watch, will fall apart quickly because it bears the stigma of Augusto's years as a cheat. Within minutes of making his pledge, the confidence man is humiliated by a former victim who recognises him and has him arrested.

IL BIDONE: Patrizia (Lorella De Luca) accepts the cheap swindler's watch from her father (Broderick Crawford).

We are our own victims if we do not
allow ourselves to trust others, be helped
by others, be ~~be~~ loved by others. "No man
134   The Cinema of Federico Fellini   is an island."

One of the reasons Fellini and his characters dread old age is because they must eventually live with the mistakes and miscalculations they made in earlier days.

When Augusto emerges from prison, he is desperate. His arrest interrupted what seems to have been his only happy moment in over a decade. His taste for companionship and its obligations was whetted at the same time as his means to appease it were destroyed. With no other alternative, Augusto returns to swindling and the lie which is becoming less and less tenable for him. Shortly thereafter, he puts his life and professional reputation on the line in what proves to be a suicidal effort to win back his daughter's confidence.

Augusto, with his new collaborators, has "taken" a peasant farmer for 350,000 lire when he suffers a peculiar tinge of conscience. In his disguise as a monsignor, he is asked to give a few consoling words to the victim's paralysed daughter. The girl is Patrizia's age and is trying her best not to be a hardship on her family. Her wish is an echo of Patrizia's reason for wanting the position as a bonded cashier—so that she will not be a burden to her mother. As Augusto listens to the story of the little girl's struggle, he becomes uneasy and appears to be moved. But it is unrealistic to believe that a man who has ruthlessly brought misery to hundreds of gullible people would be touched by the cries of a cripple. The farm girl makes him think of his own daughter and the pain his errancy has visited upon her. The paralytic's cheerfulness and appreciation of beauty leads him to consider the barrenness of his own life, and her belief in miracles spurs him to impulsive, foolhardy action. It would be a miracle for Augusto if he could redeem himself in his daughter's eyes by giving her the entire 350,000 lire she needs. In his despair and confusion he doesn't consider how Patrizia would feel about using such nefariously acquired money, nor does he weigh the unlikelihood of cheating his partners of their share of the loot. He is at the end of his rope at this point and must save himself or else face the emptiness of his life—and, thus, extinction. Predictably, when he claims that he could not bear to take the booty from the poor crippled girl's father, the rest of his team refuses to buy his sudden change of heart. They find the cash in his shoe and beat him until he is on the verge of death.

While Augusto's hardness and cruelty are in no way justifiable, they are neither an isolated phenomenon nor entirely his fault. When Picasso, Augusto and Roberto visit a slum area to collect "advance rents" for new public housing units, the state is their unseen accomplice. Many of the would-be tenants filed their applications for new apartments as long as three years earlier. Not only are they still without accommodations, but they have not even heard from the housing authority. The swindlers' lack of concern for their victims is certainly duplicated by the people who are charged with taking care of the poor. The madhouse that results when the trio starts assigning apartments is equally appalling. Each applicant is out for himself and they all virtually brawl for the privilege of being tricked by the con-artists. If these people had been able to look beyond

IL BIDONE: Augusto is, at the end, his own victim.

their own interests for a moment, they might, together, have seen through the scheme. From this sequence, one gets the impression of a society that is full of Augustos, each of whom is oblivious to everyone around him. Such a society is, on every level, unresponsive to basic human needs and unlikely to encourage its individual members to break the pattern. Outsiders of low moral resistance, especially Fellini's *vitelloni*-like provincials, are easily corrupted by this vicious cycle. This idea is developed extensively in *La dolce vita* and *8½*.

The hero of *La dolce vita* might well be one of the *vitelloni* after transplantation to Rome. (Angelo Solmi describes how the project evolved from a planned sequel to *I vitelloni* called *Moraldo in the City*.) Marcello grew up in Romagna under the sway of the values depicted in *I vitelloni*. Presumably he outgrew his childhood way of life and came to the city in search of something more stimulating. He retains some of the nature of Fausto and Alberto, including their inability to respond genuinely to anybody but themselves. Like Leopoldo, Marcello longs to be a respectable intellectual, but he grinds out only hack material. He resembles Moraldo in his passivity and lack of moral conviction. Though he is dissatisfied with his life and the state of things around him, he is unwilling to put out enough energy to correct—or even object to—whatever he feels is amiss. He simply flashes a helpless expression and lets everything go on as before.

Marcello cannot forge productive ties with other people, a problem which Fellini typically treats as the outcome of faulty communication. Marcello's world is saturated with instances of aberrant communication. He is a journalist by profession but he writes for a publication which values neither accuracy nor authenticity. His job is to distort the news by digging up dirt on celebrities and putting it into a format which will titillate his not very seriously minded readership. It is incumbent upon him never to feel sympathy for the subjects of his scandal mongering—a poise that requires a tough, mercenary approach. There is a hint of this in Marcello's smugness when he is threatened after invading the prince's privacy at the night-club. Still, Marcello is a "bleeding heart" next to his colleagues, the *paparazzi*, who are present throughout the film as a representation of what Marcello is becoming. These malignant parasites who swarm pitilessly to sites of disaster and misfortune are the nadir of honest communication. They are not above setting up a situation to provide a saleable photo and, in any case, they falsify the events they cover by misrepresenting their emotional resonances. Their lack of all principle and allegiance is well demonstrated by their attempts to goad Marcello and Sylvia's *fiancé* into an extended fray. The *paparazzi* serve as a moral zero-point against which we can judge Marcello and the people he encounters.

If there is any doubt that Marcello finds it hard to communicate, one need only observe the way he is forever talking to people who ignore him. As he dances with Sylvia, he babbles on and on about what she signifies to him, but the actress doesn't even realise that he is speaking to her. His father is so anxious to enjoy the Roman night-life that he will not stop and really converse with his son. And Maddalena makes love to another man while Marcello sits in the middle of a darkened room, pouring his soul out to her. It is not surprising that Marcello cannot get through to these people. He does not approach them as human beings, but as ideals which do not exist in the pure form that he imagines. Emma is the other side of the coin. She wants Marcello to offer her perfect middle class love, to be someone to whom she can "give her life as though he were the only man in the world." But he treats her like Sylvia, Maddalena and his father treat him, and avoids verbal exchanges with her. As with the others, he sees Emma only in terms of what she seems to offer him—endless demands— rather than as an individual with her own wants and hopes. Marcello himself is guilty of the intolerance that he finds so disheartening in others. Because he thinks only of himself, he believes that he has been let down by everyone, and that there are no valid ideals. At the beginning of the film, we see Marcello chasing an ideal, the statue of Christ, and then being unable to make the women on the roof understand him. In the end, he turns away from another ideal, Paola; this time it is he who will not hear.

The people with whom Marcello spends his time do not, themselves, make much of an effort to communicate. Most of them suffer from the same world-weariness as Marcello, only they have found some way of compensating their problem and, therefore, do not share his acute personal agitation. The aristocrats, who are supposed to be the guardians of the culture and traditions of the past, have let their trust go the way of their magnificent villa—into a state of musty deterioration. They have lost touch with the people for whom they once tried to set an example. The prince is amazed that Marcello works for a living, and the family's matriarch feigns slumber so that she won't have to talk to anyone. The common people, with the tacit encouragement of the Church, have lost their sense of spiritual community. Each looks for a miracle which will benefit his life alone. When the malicious children claim to see the Madonna under a certain tree, people trample one another to retrieve its branches. Others, like Sylvia, Maddalena and Steiner are living lies. All of these people have something valuable to offer Marcello, but they have permitted society's indifference to the individual to corrupt them. They have turned into the glossy unfeeling figures Marcello's audience wants to read about. That is why all of them—even someone as icy as Maddalena or as ridiculous as Sylvia—affect us as tragic.

Sylvia, the American movie star, is the materialisation of the mystical, earth-mother creature that haunts the childhood fantasies of many Fellini characters. Her mythological quality is stressed visually by her romp with Frankie Stout, the man who looks like a satyr. Marcello states it clearly when he tells her, "you are everything . . . You are the first woman on the first day of creation, you are the mother, the sister, the lover, the friend . . .

LA DOLCE VITA: Marcello tries to talk to Sylvia atop St. Peter's.

LA DOLCE VITA: the water shuts off in the Trevi fountain at a critical moment. For Marcello, Sylvia represents an ideal he can never attain.

an angel, the devil, the earth, the home . . . yes, that's what you are Sylvia, the home." His concept of her seems to be confirmed during her visit to the top of St. Peter's Basilica. She is carefree and enthusiastic as she dashes up the seven hundred steps to the dome. The sacred nature of the building doesn't deter her a bit; she seems above it all with her laughter and ingenuous questions. The frantic climb has the appearance of a moral triumph. None of the *paparazzi* have the stamina to complete the ascent although the actress accomplishes it effortlessly. Marcello manages, just barely, to keep up with her. By the time they walk out to the balcony, high above the city, he is huffing and puffing, having pursued her as though she were his last hope for salvation.

Sylvia, however, is not as simple and ethereal as Marcello perceives her to be. She has been used and made over by a profession which specialises in tampering with communications—the publicists. They tell her exactly how to come down the steps of the plane to milk maximum coverage of her arrival in Rome, and prompt her with provocative answers to be used at her press conference. As if to show that much of her mythological standing is trumped up, Frankie Stout, the satyr, turns out to be an opportunist who lives off wealthy widows. Even the open air night-club where they dance, in the Baths of Caracalla, is a corruption of antiquity by modern tastelessness. It is as artificial as the waiter's costume which Robert calls "a silly mixture of Roman and Phoenician," thrown together for commerical reasons. Sylvia, herself, may be genuine and spontaneous, but she is built into a world which is not.

Although Fellini shows only the public, "goddess" Sylvia, he intimates that her private life is in a state of turmoil. Her quarrel with Robert in front of the hotel establishes that she is not the free woman Marcello imagines. She has a more than casual attachment to her *"fiancé"* and is encumbered by such petty, but natural emotions as pride and jealousy. When Robert slaps her, the only protest she voices is "You shouldn't do things like that, especially in front of people." On top of everything else, she is

LA DOLCE VITA: Maddalena (Anouk Aimée), hiding behind her dark glasses, meets Marcello by chance.

LA DOLCE VITA: making love in a prostitute's bed is a form of wish fulfilment for Maddalena.

upset about her personal affairs overflowing into her public life. This is a disconcertingly trivial response for "the first woman on the first day of creation." In the early morning, after the wade in the Trevi fountain, Sylvia seems much closer to life-size than she did the night before. She may well have the protective, mothering instincts that she lavishes on the kitten, but she can never actually be the pristine vision that Marcello sees beckoning him into the pool. As soon as he physically touches her, his semi-fantasy, like the flow of water into the fountain, must cease abruptly.

If Sylvia is "the mother," Maddalena is the wife. Marcello looks upon her as a friend in whom he can confide, and at their two fortuitous meetings, he is truly pleased to see her. She has a sharp mind and shares his feeling of restlessness, if not his desperation to banish it. Because she is so impassive in everything she does, he thinks that she has faced and conquered the problem of emptiness, through a combination of strength, and her enormous wealth. Marcello hopes that she can help him achieve the same triumph.

Once again, the reality of the situation is not as Marcello understands it. Maddalena's reserve covers up her unmet need for love the way her dark sunglasses hide her bruised eye. Money and social status have not provided the relief she must have, so she resorts to a self-degrading nymphomania—a wanton parody of loving—as a means of staving off the pangs of non-fulfilment. She longs to be a whore for whom, she assumes, meaning is an irrele-

LA DOLCE VITA: Marcello's father (Anninbale Ninchi) tries to recapture his youth as he dances with a chorus girl (Magali Noel).

vancy when sex and pleasure are involved. When she fornicates in the bed of a prostitute, it is a type of wish fulfilment as well as a kinky way to abrogate boredom. "I would love to be your faithful wife," she admits to Marcello, quickly qualifying her statement with "and amuse myself like a whore at the same time." Her compulsive promiscuity is a narcotic that anaesthetises her against self-doubts. To commit herself to Marcello or anyone else would deluge her with problems which she is unwilling to face. It is much less taxing to continue in a state of moral insensibility than to tackle a new crisis of identity.

The sequence where Maddalena speaks to Marcello in the aristocrats' castle is an exercise in communicative futility. She sits in another room far down the hall from where Marcello is seated, but the trick acoustics make it sound as though she were standing by his side. Communication, for Fellini, is a prerequisite to bringing people together, but here it is used to separate the two speakers. Her mocking reference to the physical arrangement as "the chamber of serious discourse" explains her attitude toward communicating. "If I don't speak," she says, "it's as if I no longer existed." When she begins to make love with the man who enters her room she does stop speaking. Such erotic debasement removes her to an oblivion where she has no reason to be concerned about her relationship to other people.

When Marcello's father turns up in Rome, the gossip columnist tries to open lines of communication that have been closed for years. The old man's visit gives Marcello a chance to backtrack and reconsider the values which served him so well as a boy. It soon becomes obvious that these values are inadequate for an adult because they make no provision for communication. Marcello tells Paparazzo that when he was a child, his papa spent a great deal of time on the road, "I'd see him only rarely," he recalls, "and sometimes when he came back, I wouldn't recognise him." To a little boy in Romagna, a father is the head of the family, a figure of authority, the guarantee of security and little else. Marcello has never known his father as a human being, so he hopes to take advantage of the visit to get closer to him. If he can find a friend in his father, he will have established a tie that has real meaning.

After their evening together, however, Marcello and his father part, still strangers to each other. The elder Rubini is not prepared to go beyond his formal role as a father. At first he shows a proper amount of paternal concern, delivering a letter from Marcello's mother and asking his son how well his job pays. He chides Marcello for not visiting his home town occasionally and lectures him about the arrangement with Emma. Although the father is distinctly out of place in "café society," he tries to appear in control of the situation and insists upon paying the bill while naively expressing shock at its expensiveness. Mr. Rubini makes it clear that he would not feel right about speaking frankly and openly with his son when he starts hinting that he wants to go to the Kit-Kat Club, a Roman cabaret which he frequented in the Thirties. Because he is embarrassed about looking over-eager in front of his son, he broaches the matter hesitantly and obliquely, pretending that he has no first hand experience with such places. But once they arrive at the club, his reserve disappears and he is much too concerned with having a good time to pay more than token attention to Marcello. Later in the evening, Marcello becomes sullen as he begins to realise how irretrievable the complacency of his childhood is. It is impossible, at his stage of life, to regain the comforts of the family life he once knew.

Mr. Rubini's binge further demoralises Marcello by filling him with a fear of aging. The old man makes an all-out effort to recapture his youth when he tries to charm a chorus girl at the Kit-Kat. His attempt would be instantly disastrous were it not for the compassion of the dancer who is moved by him much as she is moved by Polidor's act with the balloons. The clown's evocation of loneliness makes her cry, and she detects the same sort of unhappiness behind the elder Rubini's corny banter. But even the kind attentions of the woman cannot cheer him. The excitement itself proves too much and he has an angina attack. "Do you know what makes us old?" he had asked earlier. "Boredom . . . When I sit at home I feel eighty years old." What he does not mention—even when he heads for home shattered and embarrassed—is that as one grows older, the physical capacity to enjoy frivolity seems to decline until it becomes impossible to distract oneself from the boredom. His father's mishap makes Marcello more aware of how much time he has already wasted upon ephemeral distractions and introduces a new element of urgency into his search for something durable.

Emma is certain that she can give Marcello everything he needs. But she is, in fact, offering him a closed, stifling existence, not much better than what he could have found at home in Cesena. Emma is as obtuse to his emotional needs as he is to hers and the two never really exchange ideas or feelings. There are only mutual recriminations and Emma's emotional blackmail in the form of repeated suicide attempts. During the drive to the "miracle," she insists that Marcello eat first an egg, then a banana, warning him to chew each carefully. Although he is not at all hungry, he makes only token protest, downing the snack with the resignation of a small boy who has been told to clean his plate. When they argue on a back road, toward the end of the film, neither shows the slightest desire to understand the other's position. The dispute is like a see-saw: Emma gets out of the car; Marcello implores her to get back in; Emma gets into the car and Marcello forces her to get out again. Marcello stops the car and starts the car, stops the car and starts the car. This corresponds well to the selfish on-and-off way Marcello uses Emma. He likes having her around as a back-up, a convenient refuge for times when everything goes wrong. Emma, in turn, grasps at Marcello as though she were fighting for one of the branches of the miracle tree. Her predicament is no less pressing than Marcello's, and Fellini laments the situation where two people who are so close to coming together cannot bridge the remaining ground because they will not make the effort to communicate.

There is only one person from whom Marcello is willing to learn and who will speak candidly with him, so it is ironic that Marcello never grasps what his friend Steiner is trying to tell him. Marcello reveres Steiner as a man who has built his life upon something meaningful. But, as we have seen in Chapter Two, Steiner has suppressed his real nature in favour of the discipline expected of an intellectual. This sacrifice has brought him prestige and a place of importance in the world, but it has not given him tranquillity. Marcello and Steiner are negative images of each other. Marcello feels inadequate because his life is all sensation without comprehension or reason. Steiner, on the other hand, feels cursed by the constant analysis which interferes with his ability to enjoy. The two men's brief friendship might be the intersection of the two searchlights seen from Steiner's balcony. They cross momentarily and then return to their separate corners of the sky.

Steiner has perfected a perverse habit of speech in which he expresses admiration of a person, event or object and then destroys the effect by breaking it down into its aesthetic or affective components. When Marcello admires a painting, Steiner responds with "Yes, I love it very much." Then he is compelled to say why: "The objects seem to be bathed in the light of memory, yet they're painted with such solidity and real feeling that you can almost touch them. One might say that art has left nothing to chance." In context, this final sentence is annoyingly cryptic. In line with his habit, Steiner feels duty bound to discount any experience that he cannot explain.

LA DOLCE VITA: Steiner (Alain Cuny) is an enigmatic figure as he presides over his party for intellectuals.

Although he made a recording of the sounds of nature because he "found them beautiful," he tells his guests that the tape is "nothing important." He even twists the antics of his children into an intellectual mould, praising the little boy's laughter as "understanding" and his daughter's innocent questions as poetry. Steiner then describes how sweet it is to "sleep with a little child at your side," but assures Emma that he does not allow his son to sleep with him, thus denying himself that thrill. Whenever Steiner feels himself giving in to his instinct for pleasure, he forces himself to reconsider the situation in rational terms. He has even analysed this tendency in himself, and it frightens him. "If you saw me as I see myself, you would know that I am not any taller than that," he announces, indicating about two inches. When these words are played back on a tape, they are immediately followed by a clap of thunder which gives them an ominous ring.

When Steiner talks to Marcello on the balcony, he voices misgivings about himself that he dares not discuss with the crowd in his living room. He warns his friend about the dangers of intellectual regimentation. "Any life, even the most miserable," he says, "is worth more than a sheltered existence in a world where everything is organised, where everything is practical, everything has its place." Steiner has all the elements for a peaceful, satisfying life—children, a wife, friends, honour—at his disposal. But his intellectual conditioning will not let him trust or accept such happiness at face value. From his detached point of view he can see only the depravity of the civilisation that might someday threaten his joy-filled enclave. So he disregards his own emotions and takes the only practical step—the destruction of himself and his children.

When Marcello returns to Steiner's apartment, he finds a world that is radically changed from the friendly, inviting sanctuary of the party. Steiner has shot himself and his children, and his flat has been invaded by the

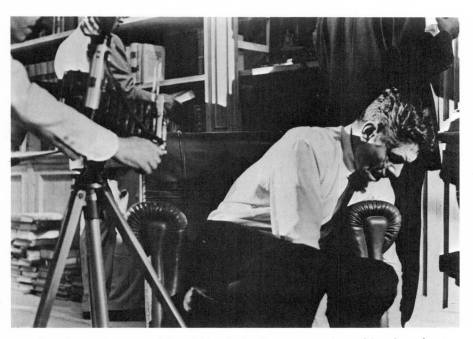

LA DOLCE VITA: after his suicide, Steiner's face reveals nothing but the fact of death.

LA DOLCE VITA: photographers gather like parasites as Marcello gives Mrs. Steiner (Renée Longarini) the news about her husband. The white buildings of EUR are in the background.

mechanical soul-lessness that scared him so much. Detectives scurry everywhere, taking precise measurements and noting the contents of the room. A reporter is calling the story in to his newspaper and embroidering his description with morbid suppositions couched in matter-of-fact language. The police photographers snap their pictures of the dead with a lack of concern that rivals that of the *paparazzi*. None of this documentation even comes close to capturing the true circumstances that led to Steiner's final act. A photograph of Steiner's face will reveal nothing more than the fact of death. When Marcello steps onto the balcony, instead of the pair of beacons hopefully piercing the darkness, there is a clear view of some of the white, geometric structures of EUR. This vista includes a hideous water tower which looks like a flying saucer or a mushroom cloud.* It is not hard to see how Steiner's paranoia would build with such monstrosities looming over his everyday life. Marcello's friend has faced his Armageddon and now his body is engulfed in the hell he dreaded.

Steiner's death stuns Marcello like nothing he has ever experienced. He had looked to the man's life as an ideal and cannot fathom why he

---

*This tower, incidentally, is identical to the one outside Vittorio's home in Antonioni's *The Eclipse*, another film which deals brilliantly with the effects of modern society upon personal communications. Antonioni seems to find the same qualities in EUR as Fellini, just as the two films, released within two years of each other, have a common outlook. After all, what are the stockbrokers of *The Eclipse* if not *paparazzi* in capitalist's clothing?

LA DOLCE VITA: corrupted communication is a theme of many of the most important Italian films of the Sixties. Both the paparazzi of LA DOLCE VITA (above) and the stockbrokers of Antonioni's ECLIPSE (below) pervert the cause of honest communication.

LA DOLCE VITA: Marcello tosses feathers over the revellers at the villa in a perfect gesture of indifference.

would kill himself and his two precious children. As the systematic madness of the apartment begins to repeat itself on the street where a dozen *paparazzi* await Mrs. Steiner, a glimmer of the truth comes through to Marcello. "Perhaps," he muses, "he was only afraid of himself . . . of us all." When Mrs. Steiner alights from her bus, still unaware of the tragedy, the *paparazzi* go wild scrambling to record her grief on film. Possibly, amidst this moral anarchy in the cold, bleached atmosphere of EUR, Marcello recalls Steiner's enigmatic words which were played back at the death scene. Steiner saw himself as standing only two inches tall in a dangerous, destruction-prone civilisation. Unable to feel or communicate truthfully, he did away with himself and those he loved. Suddenly Marcello must realise that he is certainly no bigger than the man whose example he worshiped. At this point he can either press on with his search for meaning or submit to his feeling of insignificance. The latter alternative, for a Fellini character, is as suicidal as Steiner's holding the gun to his own head and pulling the trigger. Marcello takes the easy way around this decision. He begins to lie to himself and everyone else, and tries to put the revelation of the Steiner affair out of his mind by throwing himself into a vortex of senseless debauchery.

The "orgy" sequence at the end of *La dolce vita* shows how completely Marcello sells out his search for purposeful communication. The party at the villa is the celebration of a divorce—the formal cessation of an attempt

at dialogue between a man and a woman. Marcello has renounced his liter-
ary ambitions, quit his newspaper job and joined the ranks of the professional deceivers, the public relations men. As a scandal hunting journalist, he merely exaggerated; as a celebrity press agent, his speciality is lying
—the bigger the fee, the more audacious the lie. There is no love lost among
any of the revellers and everyone is flagrantly spiteful of almost everyone
else. Marcello, now a whole-hearted participant in the hostilities rather
than just an observer, is the most contemptuous and contemptible of the
crowd. The words he uses are not meant to promote understanding, but
to humiliate. His skill at degrading others gives him an edge over them
and a false sense of superiority which he must maintain to keep himself
from focusing upon his spiritual diminutiveness. At one point, he destruc-
tively tears open a pillow and uses its feathers to insult a young woman.
Then, as each guest leaves the party, Marcello sprinkles him or her with
the feathers in a perfect gesture of casual indifference. Marcello has conceded his struggle to find an acceptable middle ground between himself
and the people who might have given him help and encouragement. He
has violated Steiner's explicit warning against taking refuge within himself.
Because he lacked resolution and was so easily turned back in his fight to
resist a society that thrives upon selfishness, he has become part of that
society and its accomplice.

8½ starts with an image which is the antithesis of the dynamic search
that runs through all but the conclusion of *La dolce vita*. We find Guido
sweltering inside a car surrounded by several lanes of motionless bumper-
to-bumper traffic. In *La dolce vita*, the automobile is a kind of *leitmotif*
alluding to the lack of any fixed points of reference in Marcello's life. He
spends an extraordinary amount of time in cars and is seen riding with
every important character in the film, save Steiner whom he believes to be
serene and settled. People pass in and out of Marcello's life like passengers
getting in and out of a vehicle. Cars, their occupants and styles of driving
become clues to Marcello's relationships. When he is with Maddalena, he
rides in her monster Cadillac which carries a prostitute in the back seat.
En route to Sylvia's press conference he follows Paparazzo's advice and
drives recklessly, cutting another car off; on the way to the "orgy" at Fregene, he drives that way without outside prompting. His fluctuating attitude toward Emma is evident in the way she bounces in and out of his
sports car during their big row. But Marcello is always moving, always trying a new possibility or, finally, speeding headlong into nothingness. Guido's
life, in contra-distinction, has stalled. Marcello is restless, but Guido is
suffocating in his own lassitude. He has nowhere to go and no means of
communicating with the people he sees spending their own pent-up lives
in neighbouring autos. Fellini elaborates on the metaphor of the cars later
when Guido and Luisa walk through an automobile showroom. There, on
the floor among the Fords, is an Indian fakir lying in a glass box. "All the
way from India," a voice on a loudspeaker announces, "see him sealed in
his glass coffin." Guido is finding it hard to breathe in his own "glass

LA DOLCE VITA: two examples of the automobile motif. Above, Marcello with Paparazzo (Walter Santesso) and a couple of chorus girls. Below, Marcello with Maddalena and the prostitute (Adriana Moneta).

coffin" with its closed windows and locked doors, so he struggles frantically to escape.

The traffic snarl is part of a dream which is a blueprint for the rest of *8½*, save the finale. After pounding on the body of his automotive prison, Guido escapes, almost magically. But instead of trying to reach the people in the other cars, he floats into the air over a gridwork structure which, we will later learn, has been built at his behest though he has yet to think of a use for it. Symbolically, then, it represents the gargantuan expectations that everyone has for Guido and his current inability to meet them. The Guido of the dream bypasses this tower and soars ecstatically out to the sea, near where he spent his boyhood. But just as he has regained the freedom of this place, he notices that his leg is tied to a rope by which two men on the beach are manipulating him like a kite. This aspect of the fantasy will be clarified in the memory of his days at the farmhouse when one of the women taking care of him pulls back a bedsheet to reveal a large kite in the place of the boy Guido. The two men give the rope a tug and the flying figure plunges toward the earth. When the dream ends, Guido acts it out again and again: whenever the pressures of his adult world start closing in on him he contemplates—either through memories or an interlude of fantasy—how much less complicated things were when he was a child in the provinces.

Guido feels that, like the tie-up on the street, everything has come to a standstill for him. He is hemmed in on all sides by the demands that so many people are making of him. His mistress, Carla, simply refuses to let herself be shut away in a dark corner where she can be taken out for use at Guido's whim. Luisa, his wife, baulks at having to take care of a man who expects continuous consideration and attention, but will not reciprocate. When these two women ask for help with their own needs, Guido has no answer to give them and consequently, would rather not speak with them. He pretends to be asleep when Luisa enters their hotel room after visiting the rocket ship, and he hides behind a newspaper when Carla shows up at the same café as he and his wife.

His personal impasse is duplicated in his professional activities. Guido is in pre-production for a film he is to direct and his staff, cast and backers are waiting for him to make decisions that will get the project rolling. Again, the film-maker is not at all sure of what to do, so he bluffs and procrastinates, hoping to buy time. If he can delay everybody long enough, he figures, his inspiration will return and the answers will come to him. Guido does not care to admit that his private life is the well-spring of his artistic power and that his problems with the production are a manifestion of his stalemate with Carla and Luisa. If he cannot express himself on the most fundamental level, how can he hope to do so as an artist on the public screen?

Rather than starting at the roots of his lethargy and trying to put his marital situation in order, Guido tries to impose his director's prerogative upon those who supposedly love him. Carla obliges him in this pretention

8½: Carla (Sandra Milo) and Guido make love in Carla's hotel room.

up to a point. She lets him make her up like a whore, dictate her facial expressions and entrances, and follows the scenario of his erotic fantasy. She is well suited to the role and easily satisfies Guido's appetite for sheer carnality. With her clothes on, however, Carla is too mindless for him to associate with, yet he does not have the option of sending her away until he is ready for her next scene. His mistress has feelings of her own and, contrary to what Guido may believe, is not sneaking out on her husband because of a vocation to serve the film-maker. She wants him to love her— "Guido, do you love me a little?" she asks, like Gelsomina to Zampano— and feels that he can give her something that her own spouse cannot. At the spa, Guido tries to keep Carla out of his hair by lodging her at an out of the way hotel and leaving her to her own devices. She retaliates, not entirely without spite, by forcing her lover to take notice of her when she shows up at embarrassing times or makes herself ill with mineral water. Guido understands these escapades not as the actions of an unhappy woman, but as annoyances that interfere with his own plans.

Guido's image of Luisa, too, is entirely a function of what she means to him. When he looks at her, he sees only her severity. The woman he screen tests for the wife in his film is straight-laced and astringent; her most striking feature is a pair of unattractive shell glasses like those the real Luisa wears. In the harem fantasy, when all the women Guido knows behave as he wishes they would, Luisa is a much softer person, as well as the

8½: Guido, wearing his school uniform, helps his father (Annibale Ninchi) back into the grave.

most tolerant and self-sacrificing of the wives. She doesn't join the general rebellion, but continues, in work clothes, with the preparation of the master's dinner. She keeps order, makes no demands, and looks after Guido's comfort like the old grandmother who took care of him in the farmhouse when he was small. But neither Guido's ideal for Luisa nor his actual impression of her does her justice. While he tries so hard to mould her into something she is not, he overlooks her sensitivity and spiritedness. When they dance together on the restaurant terrace, she is so happy that she repeats Cabiria's performance with the actor and separates from her husband to do a little step on her own. As with Cabiria, this impulsive movement reflects vitality and spontaneity. In addition, it pinpoints Luisa as an independent focus of animation, a complete being who should not be eclipsed by her husband.

Guido's dealings with Carla and Luisa are limited by his attraction to his childhood which asserts itself in two antagonistic, though equally debilitating ways. On one hand, Guido longs for the amenities of childhood—the doting attentions of one's elders and freedom from responsibility—as an antidote to the pressures that are building up around him. On the other hand, he still feels the effects of the moral restrictions forced upon him by his upbringing, especially his Catholic education. Neither the lack of obligation nor the arbitrary morality are compatible with his current circumstances. But his childish vanity has prevented him from finding his proper

8½: "Don't you know Saraghina is the devil?" the priest asks the boy Guido in the confessional.

place among those who are his equals. He has never reconciled his past with his present.

When Guido sleeps with Carla, he dreams that his dead mother comes to clean the wall of their hotel room, as though she were attempting to scrub away the shame of the whole liason. He feels her stern disapproval there as much as he did after the priests caught him watching Saraghina's suggestive rhumba. Guido looks to Carla for the same sort of arousal he found in Saraghina, so while he remains in the shadow of his school days, he continues to feel guilty about his need for pleasure. With Saraghina, his mother was disgraced on his account; with Carla, it is Luisa who is hurt. In his dream, then, he confuses the two women, bending to kiss his mother who is suddenly transformed into his wife. "Don't you recognise me?" Luisa asks; then, accusingly, she demands, "What were you thinking about?" The dream also localises another point of entanglement between the two periods of Guido's life. At the imaginary reunion, his parents are unexpectedly distant. His father has nothing more important to tell him than what comes out in small talk about the height of his crypt's roof. He offers only fatherly disappointment when the producer indicates that Guido is not living up to everyone's hopes for him. Guido was no closer to his father than Marcello was to his, and this poverty of warmth and understanding between the boy and his parents has carried over to his marriage.

A wife, like a mother or a father, has a well defined place in Guido's thinking. He has no idea of how to handle a relationship that exceeds these bounds.

The church, too, is a restraint from Guido's boyhood which retards his development as an adult. It was the priests who placed Saraghina in league with the devil and who, with their painful and humiliating punishment, sought to ensure that Guido would never again be comfortable in the company of Saraghina-like women. In doing this they further impeded his capacity to accept people for what they are rather than what they represent. The advance man for the cardinal criticises the cinema for its free mingling of "sacred" and "profane" love and, during the imaginary visit to the steam bath *cabana*, the prelate intones that "all that is not of the city of God is of the city of the devil." Guido went back to see Saraghina, even after receiving a severe reprimand, just as he continues to see Carla three years after he and Luisa vented his extramarital activities. But he expects censure for such deviations from what he has been taught—if not from his mother or the church, then from his wife. It is unlikely that he will ever be happy under such conditions but, according to the church, it is not his task on earth to be happy. Others think they can turn to the cardinal and his institution for whatever they need—a Mexican divorce, financial success, anything. However, the cardinal is isolated and protected from the realities of day-to-day emotional life. He is not even vaguely concerned with the tensions of those to whom he ministers. Indeed, he offers homilies like those hammered into Guido at school, which only increase his agitation.

Different people take Guido's attachment to his childhood in different ways, none of them favourable. Luisa's sister is repelled by the director's childishness and Rosella, just before the harem sequence, asks Guido if he will ever grow up. Daumier, the critic, finds his collaborator's nostalgic tendencies to be the source of undesirable ambiguity in his work, a cause of murky thinking. This is also the view of Pace who, in one of his more alert moments, recognises that Guido, in his screenplay, is looking at the confusion within himself. This, the producer cautions, is making the work vague and generally incomprehensible.

Luisa, understandably, is much less charitable than the others. She is the person most directly touched by Guido's evasions and self-indulgences and she finds him wilful—a "liar" and a "fraud." His most literal lying is his denial of any ongoing involvement with Carla. This is a specific instance of his general refusal to open his life to Luisa—to let her know what is perturbing him and why. Guido shows Luisa only those things about himself that he thinks she should know in order to discharge her duties as his wife; matrimony to him is a matter of servitude, not of sharing or union. He has no compunctions against publicising a slanted version of their most intimate secrets as long as it will show him in a favourable light. Luisa was hurt when she learned of the stories about their marriage that he had confided in Carla, but she is absolutely mortified when she sees his screen test for the wife in his film. As Fellini cuts between the actress on the screen

8½: Marcello and Luisa (Anouk Aimée), more estranged than ever, await the train which will take them away from the production site. This scene is the prelude to the dining car ending and does not appear in the finished film.

and Luisa in the audience, the unfairness of Guido's publicly flaunted impression of his wife becomes unmistakable. The actress in the clip being projected is composed and rational as she tells her husband that he can have his freedom. The footage pictures her as a bitchy, harping woman who is fed up with not being able to dominate her spouse. But the real Luisa, sitting in her chair, is moved to tears by the test. The painfulness of the screening ordeal is evident in her embarrassed fidgeting with her collar and her hurt, choked-up expression. To spare herself further humiliation, she feigns equanimity and leaves the auditorium. Outside, Luisa rails against the way Guido has treated her both on film and in their marriage. To an outsider she might, at this moment, seem as shrewish as the woman in the screen test. But that piece of film showed no trace of the long-standing emotional torment that underlies her outburst. The comparison between the real wife and the wife on screen supports Luisa's charge that Guido shows others only what suits him—only the things that make him look wonderful.

Claudia offers the most incisive appraisal of Guido. She reacts to his description of the protagonist of his upcoming film—obviously Guido himself—with a discernible lack of sympathy. "I don't feel sorry for a man like that at all," she says. "It's all his own fault. Why should he expect anything of anyone else . . . He doesn't know how to love." When she realises that there is no part for her in the film, she calls Guido "a swindler"—not out of anger, but as though it were a foregone conclusion.

Not knowing how to love—how to communicate honestly—is the heart of Guido's troubles. He is roundly criticised for never making love stories. Agostini's two nieces chortle over his deficiency in this area and the question, "Why don't you make love stories?" is asked again and again. Although the question is just one of many banal things that reporters commonly ask a director, the query has special significance for Guido. A man can say nothing about a subject of which he is ignorant, so obviously a man who doesn't know how to love cannot be expected to make movies about love.

Just as Guido has no answers for the journalists who hound him, he has nothing to tell Luisa, Carla, Pace, Daumier or any of the production staff whose work hinges upon his collaboration. In fact, Guido rarely says anything of consequence to anybody. When he speaks, other than during one of his reveries, it is usually to ask a question or to avoid having to answer one. His self mocking comment beneath the spaceship scaffolding tells the whole story of why his career—and his marriage—have become derailed. "I really have nothing to say," he chants, "but I'm going to say it anyway." The only way to do this is to fabricate—to lie—and everyone, from his wife to the newsmen who represent the public are becoming sick of Guido's lies.

What kind of options does Guido have in this crisis? His film is to be based upon his own life and he tells Claudia that it begins with a weak,

8½: Gloria (Barbara Steele) and Mezzabota (Mario Pisu) cavort on the terrace at the spa.

tired man who is unsure of himself, who wants to possess and consume everybody. Therefore, the solution to Guido's artistic problem must also be the solution to his personal problem. Inspiration means self-revitalisation, a renewal of his ability to communicate on all levels.

The most attractive alternative, as Guido sees it, is escape into the past or into fantasy. This solution would obviate the need to communicate. Guido has even gone as far as making provision for such a getaway in his film. The spaceship, we are told, will carry the people in the movie away from a barren, ravaged Earth to a better home on another planet. But anyone who is casually familiar with the content of the film will readily detect the incongruity of this piece of machinery. Guido, himself, is at his wits' end trying to think of a way to fit the launching platform into the picture. This expensive self-indulgence is as responsible as any other physical factor for holding up production. There is no conceivable place for the contrivance in the movie, just as there is no realistic means for Guido to run away from his dilemma. The blast-off is to be rendered by special effects, superimposing a model rocket and the tower. In other words, it is to be a cinematic lie. Similarly, Guido's daydreams of a place where everything is as he orders it to be are lies to himself. He must continue in his present rut until he scraps both the spaceship housing and his escapist fantasies.

Another possibility that Guido contemplates is separation from Luisa. That notion is encouraged by Mezzabota who is Guido's senior, but who seems rejuvenated since he left his wife of thirty-one years to take up with one of his daughter's friends from school. Guido is feeling more aged and infirm than ever—Claudia observes that he dresses like a man of eighty and Conocchio warns him that he is getting old—so Mezzabota's new-found youth is most attractive to him. But what could Guido do if he and Luisa went their separate ways? Someone like Mezzabota's girl-friend, Gloria, a malignant intellectual who is even more dishonest than Guido, would not give him happiness. And as long as he insists upon defining roles for the people in his life, a change of partners will not bring about any improvement. The fault to be corrected lies with Guido, not with his choice of spouse.

At the end of *8½*, Guido actually tries two different ways out of his quandry. Just as he has conceded to himself and Claudia that there is no film, Connochio and Pace show up to tell him about a gala press conference to be held the next morning by the spaceship. There he will be expected to answer questions about his forthcoming film—or, rather, to admit to a hostile gathering of reporters that he is washed up, a phony. As the cars pull up to the press conference site, they recall the traffic jam which opened *8½*. Guido is dragged forcibly to the microphones where he is to make his self-annihilating confession. Trying to put it off, he again resorts to lying. "Tomorrow," he promises, but Pace insists that his director proceed with the announcement. The journalists seem bent upon destroying him, screaming abusive questions which frequently strike at the core of his insecurity; "Why do you think your life should be of interest to anybody

8½: Guido, after reconciling himself with his past, directs the people who have figured in his life around a huge circus ring.

else?" "Don't you take yourself too seriously?" "Don't you think communication is the trouble with the modern world?" "Why don't you make love stories?" One gloating woman turns toward the camera and sneers, "He's lost. He has nothing to say." Finally he sees Luisa standing by the table in her wedding dress; "Won't you ever really marry me?" she implores. But as the full impact of the loss of his wife strikes him for the first time, the reporters chime in aggressively on Luisa's theme, screeching questions like "What does your wife think about all this?" Instead of admitting that with his ego deflated he is nobody—a virtual suicide—he crawls under the table and shoots himself in the forehead. Cancelling his picture about his life is analogous to his killing himself, and this is the first alternative Fellini shows us.

With his project abandoned, Guido feels truly alone and insignificant. The spaceship scaffolding, his base for escape, is coming down when his desolation suddenly vanishes and he understands the error he has been making all along. The master of ceremonies from Maya's mind-reading act appears in front of Guido's car and begs him not to leave just yet. The top-hatted entertainer is an old friend of Guido's and here acts as a benevolent medium between past and present. Under his influence Guido sees the white Claudia, the ideal, raise her head and smile at him. Then he pictures various figures from the different stages of his life. The ideal walks away from Guido—he no longer needs her—while everyone else moves toward him, apparently through the good offices of the energetic master of cere-monies. Among the people who join this crowd is the boy Guido, dressed in an all white variation of his school uniform. The washed-up director himself then takes control and signals the child to open a curtain in front of the spaceship tower. All the people whom Guido had tried to turn into functionaries of his own conceit come marching down from the tower on this cue and join hands as part of a continuous human chain—the chain of Guido's life. The people who comprise the chain are not really any different from the way we have seen them before. Pace still looks like he is talking big business and Carla is as giddy as ever. Guido calls to his mother, but she just gestures hopelessly, still refusing to forgive the son who shamed her. The cardinal is as frail as in the steambath, but Guido kisses his ring without reservation. Although Luisa expresses doubt about her husband's wanting to start over again, she re-enters the stream of his life anyway. This time, however, she has reason for optimism in that Guido takes her hand and they join the line as a pair. He has acknowledged the importance of all these people—both friends and antagonists—in his life, and is finally willing to accept them for what they are, and for the contri-bution they have made to what he is. The inverse also holds: because he appreciates each of the men and women who make up his life he accepts himself. "I am what I am and not what I want to be," he proclaims. We have seen Guido move from narcissism to a state in which he has no self-esteem whatever. In this final sequence, he recognises that there is a middle ground where he can still have pride and confidence in himself while ad-mitting his mutual dependence on others.

Guido has also learned to live with his confusion. Even though he is still uncertain of what he is seeking in his art and in his being, he is reassured by his having an important place in the procession. Guido had set himself apart from those whom he now sees as individuals in the continuum of his life. The key to self-realisation, he discovers, is to join these people as an equal. This is the identity with respect to other people that Fellini heroes from Gelsomina to Giulietta have tried to establish for themselves. The movie ends with little Guido playing alone under the spotlight which fades as he marches off to join the others. Guido, we take it, has successfully isolated his childhood experience and reconciled it with his immediate needs.

It is immaterial whether this epilogue is taken as a "happy ending" in which Guido's tribulations magically melt away permitting him to finish his film, or as a convenient flight of fantasy like the harem sequence. Fel-lini here is emphasising his conviction that Guido is not irretrievably lost—

that it is within his power to reverse his frustrating isolation. Fellini had originally planned to end *8½* with Guido making the same discovery he makes in the release version of the film, only the bolt would strike him as he rode in a dining car with Luisa. In a subjective shot from Guido's seat, he would see all the people in his life sitting at the other tables in the coach. Although it is generally futile to guess with hindsight how an out-take might have worked in a film, it would seem (judging from the description of the discarded sequence in Deena Boyer's "The 200 Days of *8½*"[3]) that this ending would have left Guido at a crossroads. Since the occupants of the car would have been seen from Guido's perspective, he would not have appeared in the shot. Thus he would still have to make the decision of whether or not to join these phantoms and continue moving forward with them. The film would have concluded on a note of hopeful uncertainty. The ending that was used seems much more suitable if only because it is definite about Guido's chances to rectify his life and gives us a taste of the exhilaration that he will find should he do so. Also, because

8½: Fellini sits pensively in the dining car set that was built for the alternative ending of the film.

his future depends upon his willingness to change a deeply ingrained attitude, his reclamation is conditional and the ending that was used properly presents his change of spirit in the subjunctive mood.

The endings of *8½* and *Juliet of the Spirits* are the culmination of the search begun by Moraldo in *I vitelloni* and continued, with varying success, by Gelsomina, Cabiria, Augusto and Marcello. All of them have to strike a balance between themselves and the people they need. The female characters tend to go overboard in turning themselves over to the men they want to love them, while the males indulge in self-aggrandisement at the expense of those they need to love. Fellini does not necessarily blame his characters for the predicaments in which they find themselves. He recognises that they are subject to the deleterious influences in the church, parochialism and modern society, and to the basic human trait of clinging to whatever one finds comfortable. But he does feel that the responsibility for overcoming these obstacles lies with the individual alone. One must recognise the relative value of each part of one's life without becoming obsessed with any single phase of it. There must also be a personal commitment to honest communication. Gelsomina dies when she loses her ability to communicate and her faith that everything she is doing is worthwhile. By the same token Zampano softens only when he comprehends her importance to him. Cabiria breaks into a smile when she finds that one of the great tragedies of her life has, as a happy side-effect, changed her circumstances. Marcello and Augusto both destroy themselves with self-serving lies. Only Guido and Giulietta really come close to reclamation when they can accept themselves and everyone they have known without compromising anyone.

5

Questioning the Past

In *8½*, one is never sure whether Guido is literally planning a movie about himself or whether Fellini is declaring that any genuine work of art will incorporate the full being of the artist. The film works equally well under either interpretation, so this point of ambiguity is of interest primarily as an indicator of where Fellini himself is heading. After laying open and exploring so much of his own life through Guido, it is not surprising that Fellini soon abandoned proxy characters altogether. In *I clowns* and *Roma*, Fellini turns up in person and bluntly states that he intends to sift and examine some of the pieces of his life. This kind of study is also implied in *Amarcord* with its memories of Romagna and its broad character base. In these three films we are watching a man as he confronts and reconciles himself with his past. It is as if Fellini were trying to turn Guido's extravagant final vision into a reality for himself. This move is daring because it puts Fellini's honesty to a rigorous public trial. Guido could hide behind the hypothetical hero of his film when he explained himself to Claudia, but in *Roma*, *I clowns* and *Amarcord* Fellini is baring himself—flaws and virtues alike—before an international audience. The audacity of such an effort is overwhelming and it has offended a significant portion of the world's film critics (presumably many of the same people who felt that the ending of *8½* was glib and artificial.) In putting forward his preferences and prejudices, the director does not always come across in a favourable light. But it is always stimulating to watch the complaints, confessions and loves of one of the most imaginative and observant men in the cinema.

Of the three films *I clowns* is the least adventurous as an attempt at introspection. Fellini purportedly sets out to discover what, if anything remains of the circus, the primordial spectacle of his boyhood upon which he has built his film career. "Is the naïvety of the public gone?" he asks, wondering if his entire approach to life is based upon the misconceptions of a child. At first he hints that the answer may be affirmative. The first circus to be visited is approached slowly as though we were penetrating another dimension or another galaxy. As the camera glides past the sparkling lights, there is no synchronous sound, only the theme from *8½* playing slowly,

163

I CLOWNS: Fellini stages a mock funeral to prove that the clown is not dead.

distantly, on the soundtrack. Later we pass a circus building which has been converted to other uses and hear a taxi driver speak derisively of the institution. Despite these signs of atrophy, Fellini's initial query— his challenge to himself— proves to have been rhetorical. He has been certain of his answer all along; the circus and its clowns are as vital as they have ever been. So in *I clowns* Fellini is merely justifying his way of looking at the world and not really questioning it at all.

Roma is not nearly as calculated as *I clowns*. Instead of trying to defend his feelings about himself and his past, Fellini states them forthrightly and without embarrassment over what his audience may think of his attitudes. While shooting in Villa Borghese, Fellini is cornered by students on one side and a middle-aged lawyer on the other, each faction complaining about his film for conflicting reasons. Fellini makes no apologies for what he is doing because *Roma* is to be more a film about himself than one about the city.

Fellini does not project a very attractive image of himself in *Roma*. In many respects he is reminiscent of Guido in his most self-pitying frame of mind. Fellini, however, is not obsessed with his provincial childhood, which he now sees as a period of limited possibilities, but with the life he knew in the Forties when everything seemed promising and exciting. One can easily appreciate his enthusiasm over the bustling train station and the teeming *trattoria* in Via Albalonga. And while the people he meets in the music-hall and *pensione* are no more incredible than the strange types he knew at home, there are so many more of them in such infinite variety. But Fellini, as we see him in *Roma*, is disgusted and disquieted by the changes that have brought prewar Rome into its present state. His fear of the new values undermining and displacing the old ones is metaphorically expressed in the hallucinatory underground sequence which might be considered the film's centrepiece. In this episode, workmen using science fiction like machines to dig the city's new subway line unearth an ancient Roman house, complete with frescoes, tile pools and perfectly preserved sculpture. As the workmen marvel at their discovery, the external air from above penetrates the excavation and the entire structure crumbles to dust. Some of Fellini's specific points are well taken—the ugliness of the Raccordo Annulare highway, for example—while others seem to be the product of a middle-aged man bemoaning the passing of a way of life that he once enjoyed.

Fellini's treatment of the "hippies" is his most flagrant dismissal of a phenomenon he does not understand. "I had such hope for the hippie movement," Fellini said shortly after the *premiere* of *Roma*. "Remember, I lived through Fascism and here was a group of people to which those ideas were completely foreign. But look at them? What are they doing? Where are they going?"** But Fellini's use of the counter-culture in *Roma* seems less a matter of philosophical condemnation than an expression of

ROMA: Fellini's crew explores the Roman house unearthed in the subway excavation.

fear. He shows the young people virtually taking over the Spanish Steps like a herd of animals. He comments in amazement at the open character of their lives together, and then begins to muse about the days when one had to sneak out to a whorehouse for sex. Shortly thereafter, in Trastevere, he links the "hippies" with chaos as they battle a squadron of police in the piazza. Among those who dine complacently in the adjacent café as this conflict rages are two people who have figured importantly in Fellini's life in Rome—Marcello Mastroianni and Alberto Sordi. Sordi, along with the other diners, is actually enjoying the fracas in the centre of the square. The people at the tables are Fellini's generation and they would prefer not to be involved with the new turmoil in their midst.

Although one may be inclined to take violent issue with Fellini over his point of view in *Roma*, it does not seem right to censure him for it. The director is still a far cry from the princess of the black aristocracy who spends her time wishing that the days of Pius XII would return. Nor does Fellini suffer from Guido's dishonesty which, as Luisa remarked, is a matter of sparing no one in order to make himself look wonderful in the public's eyes. In owning up to his narrowmindedness, Fellini is discovering some of the inconsistencies in his way of looking at things. Inherent in the Trastevere segment is a criticism of Fellini's own position apropos of the "hippies." There is clearly something barbaric in the well-to-do onlookers' smugness and lack of concern over the vicious clubbings taking place just beyond their tables. In the finished film, this aspect of the situation far outweighs the director's dread of the new element of disorder in the city. By stating his problems, anxieties and inhibitions candidly on film, Fellini seems to work through them and is able to recognise them for what they are.

In this vein, it is interesting to note the progressive changes in Fellini's treatment of his days in Romagna as he moves from the often warmhearted remembrances of *I vitelloni* to the hostile satire of *Amarcord*. In *I vitelloni*, Fellini is kindly disposed toward the overgrown babies of the town, their relatives and acquaintances. When Moraldo moves on, into an uncertain future, the last glimpses of those he leaves behind are appealingly tranquil. Despite these people's limitations, one wishes them well. Moraldo—if we may extrapolate him into Guido and Marcello—will look back upon his hometown as a place of peacefulness and familiarity, especially when he is troubled. This is the dominant impression he will carry away with him, and it must coincide with Fellini's sentiments toward Rimini in 1953.

But as Fellini scrutinises himself and his personal history through several films, his thinking undergoes a series of gradual modifications until his perspective has significantly altered. He arrives at the same conclusion that Guido and Giulietta reach in the codas of their respective films: figures from the past have been a major influence in making him what he is today, but he has outgrown their hold over him and is now changing under the sway of the people and ideals that are important to him at present. The differences in his films, Fellini is fond of saying, are the differences of "a man at different seasons of his life. The way you look at yourself now is not the way you looked at yourself when you were a boy, and the way you looked at yourself as a boy ten years ago is not the way you look at your boyhood today. There is no past, only an effect on the present. You can remember what the past was, but what is important is what it means now."**

In *Amarcord*, Fellini is looking at his past from a point which, for him, is unusually distant in time and space. Although he cannot dissociate himself completely from the world in which he grew up, he is now able to look back upon it with a lucidity and detachment not found in his other reconstructions of Romagna. In *I vitelloni*, our impressions of both the pleasantness and inadequacy of provinciality emanate from Moraldo, the prototype of several of Fellini's semi-autobiographical characters. In *Roma, I clowns* and *Fellini: A Director's Notebook*, there are stand-ins for Fellini at earlier ages, and we see everything from their points of view. But there is not a single character in *Amarcord* whom one can comfortably place as Fellini, either young or old. The occasional narrator, the lawyer with the bicycle, offers a picture of the town that is full of subjective misrepresentations. His harangues are inevitably undermined by the local clowns who harass him during these presentations, and by the vignettes we are shown. His foolishness makes the business of defending and clinging to the past appear highly suspect. Titta is a rather coarse young man who bears no physical resemblance whatever to the director. While the film generally focuses on him and his family, he is often—as in the Fascist celebration— just one of many participants. If some of his experiences fall in line with those Fellini has recounted in previous films, it is because there is not a lot of variability from one life to the next in the provinces. Thus Titta, while an individual in his own right, is more a representative specimen than a source of perceptions. *Roma, I clowns* and *I vitelloni* are pictures of a particular place in terms of what it meant to Fellini at the time he lived there. As such they tend to be fond recollections. *Amarcord* is a portrait of Fellini's first home as he sees it from where he stands today. Nostalgia has nothing to do with these memories.

The village in *Amarcord* is even more isolated and self-contained than the one in *I vitelloni*, as indicated by the closed cycle of the seasons. The *manine*, tiny bits of airborne fluff, herald the arrival of spring at the beginning and end of the film, and both times their appearance is acknowledged with a celebration. The first spring is welcomed with a festival which includes massive bonfires, as though the remnants of the past year were being destroyed to make way for a fresh start. The spring which caps the film sees Gradisca's wedding—a ceremony that is popularly regarded as a new beginning. But in this case, the nuptials represent the end of a dream. The voluptuous Gradisca has been the object of the sexual fantasies of nearly every male in town. They regularly fabricate stories about her, gaze lasciviously after her, and try to sneak up from behind in order to touch a choice part of her anatomy. Titta himself cannot resist trying his luck and slides into the seat next to hers at the Fulgor cinema. He timidly places his hand on her knee only to receive a cold stare in return. Most fantastic

AMARCORD: Gradisca's wedding to a local carabiniere *marks the end of her dreams of glamour.*

of all is the legend of how she offered herself to a visiting prince to obtain a favour for a local official. Her marriage to a balding, middle-aged *cara-biniere* finishes off one of the major, albeit dubious, sources of excitement for the townspeople. The respectable, but ordinary match also puts an end to Gradisca's fantasies. After years of dreaming about Gary Cooper while sitting alone in the Fulgor, she accepts what promises to be a thoroughly unglamorous existence. Gradisca's fortunes are characteristic of the town's life which is based upon illusory thrills that come and go like the seasons, leaving nothing of value or permanance. The inhabitants sustain themselves upon these illusions, so when one fades, it is quickly replaced by another of equal inconsequentiality.

Some of these phenomena are literally seasonal. Every autumn the people line the road for the Mille Miglia auto races. They wait half the night for the payoff—the roar of the engines and a pair of headlights streaking past them. The event fires a number of private fantasies. Titta imagines himself winning the competition and, consequently, the admiration of everybody's dream girl, Gradisca. Ciccio, in his mind's eye, gives the girl who despises him her comeuppance. But the only lasting remnant of the evening's commotion is the ear of a dog that was run over by one of the speeding vehicles. Equally as ephemeral is the summer season at the Grand Hotel which brings out the braggarts and gigolos to take advantage of the holiday centre of cosmopolitanism. They dance with the wealthy foreign women and make passes at them. Regardless of their success, the men will later inflate their little adventures into versions which will titilate their *vitelloni* friends. After the establishment closes for the winter, the schoolboys longingly pantomime a glorious evening of dancing on its terrace. The building is the inspiration for countless legends and tall tales like Biscien's escapade with the concubines or Gradisca's "white-telephone"—like intrigue with the prince.

The townsfolk's dependence upon transient illusions is typified by the passage of the giant transatlantic ocean liner, "Rex." When the ship sails within a few miles of the coast, the entire population takes to the sea in rowboats to catch a glimpse of the fabled monster. Like all the other attractions, the "Rex" will slip by in the darkness, causing a flurry of emotion, after which the onlookers will return to their normal, empty lives. The "Rex" is an ideal to them, a massive, impressive accomplishment, and in the night, on the vast open sea, the spectators see it as an incredible phantom. As it goes on its way it carries with it all the excitement and romance

AMARCORD: The "Rex" is a phantom that passes in the night. It represents all the silly aspirations of the townspeople.

AMARCORD: Titta slides his hand up Grandisca's leg in the Fulgor cinema.

that they will never find—try as they may—in the Mille Miglia, the Grand Hotel or their other plebeian endeavours.

It is natural to look sympathetically upon people who do not realise how useless and limited their lives are. This is part of the reason why characters like Fausto and Alberto in *I vitelloni* and Checco in *Variety Lights* are capable of moving us. It is also possible to find some warm laughter for an innate clown like Ivan Cavalli when he discovers that his silly ambitions are being wrecked by his romantic wife. But many of the denizens of *Amarcord*, though funny in a vulgar way, inspire no love at all in us. Such utterly distasteful individuals as Il Patacca, Zeus the headmaster, and the Gerarca, to name a few, are unheard of in Fellini's features through *Juliet of the Spirits*, and rare in *Roma* and *I clowns*. In fact, the few unredeemed types in the later films are either sinister like the mutilated war veteran, or pushy and authoritarian, like the stationmaster or the man in the bomb shelter. These qualities abound in the characters of *Amarcord*. Il Patacca, Titta's uncle, is a foul, destructive man whose pranks such as stranding Giudizio atop the bonfire, are maliciously cruel. "Zeus," like most of the teachers under his direction, is humourless, tyrannical and, one suspects, desirous of preserving his dignity at any cost. Il Gerarca del Borgo, the local Fascist leader, is no less aware of his position of importance. He walks with a swagger, a kind of parade of self-confidence, and generally lords it over those

AMARCORD: the town's most important people run down the corso—*like children playing a game—when the Federale pays a visit.*

whom he passes in the street. Even with his retinue on the terrace of the Grand Hotel, his bearing is nothing less than imperious. Gigino Penna Bianca, one of the *vitelloni* who preys upon foreign women at the Grand Hotel, is as vain as he is opportunistic. None of these people have done anything to justify their conceit; they simply assume their own superiority and behave accordingly. To varying degrees, most of the people of the town have equivalent delusions about themselves, from Gradisca to the Ronald Colman look-alike manager of the Fulgor to Titta himself. In these attitudes Fellini sees the roots of an empty, dangerous, intolerant chauvinism. When an entire community is ensconced in stupid, childish illusions, Fascism can easily thrive. There is a clear connection then between the two events which really electrify the city—the passing of the "Rex" and the Fascist rally on the 21st of April.

Virtually everybody turns out for the Fascist show, gathering first at the train station to meet the *Federale*. It is as if they were all taking part in a grandiose fantasy. Gradisca becomes semi-hysterical when she lays eyes upon the *Federale*. "I have to touch him. Let me touch him," she screams. The Lawyer, our upright narrator-historian, praises the greatness of the Roman heritage and Il Patacca, who is among the militia, calls out to the Federale, "All I have to say is this: Mussolini's got two balls this big!" The teachers who pompously exercise such authority over their classes now march with

AMARCORD: The Grand Hotel brings a touch of cosmopolitanism to the provincial town.

the important Fascists. "Zeus" runs along the *corso* with the uniformed dignitaries and the maths teacher, leading the *Donne Italiane* ecstatically exhorts the marvels of the political movement that is "rejuvenating" the country. The crowning touch for the day is the raising of a monstrous portrait of Mussolini rendered in red and yellow flowers. The likeness is imposing, stylised and so ugly that it seems ironic that it is made from flowers which are usually associated with beauty. The excitement sends Titta's schoolmate, Ciccio, into a daydream in which he marries Aldina with the approval of the towering face. The day's rituals are no less absurd than the pilgrimage to the "Rex," indeed, the two spectacles fulfil exactly the same needs for the townspeople.

Throughout the 21st of April festivities, everyone behaves idiotically. Their deportment is on the same level as the foolishness we observed in the schoolrooms. In children and teenagers such nonsense is not only expected, but often amusing. In adults, however, it is disturbing and unacceptable. The teachers, though more pretentious, seem no more mature than their charges, and this state of arrested adolescence extends to the entire town.

One incident graphically demonstrates what happens when infantile antics become the norm for adults. After a record player blaring out the "Internationale" is shot to pieces by the Fascists, Il Gerarca has Titta's father brought to headquarters. He accuses the father of planting the device in the bell tower and then gleefully forces the old man to drink glass after glass of castor oil. The Fascists take the same sort of delight in this stunt that Titta's friends take in urinating from the balcony of the cinema. When such malice becomes the accepted standard for those with public responsibility, it is not far from forcing ingestion of a purgative to the burn torture of *Open City*.

The preponderance of contemptible characters in *Amarcord* does not mark a change or inconsistency in Fellini's fundamental values. Although he is viewing familiar material in a new way—which accounts for the difference in *Amarcord's* tone as compared to earlier works—he still voices tremendous concern for the welfare of the individual. Titta, he notes with profound sadness, is destined to go the way of the others in the town since it is unlikely that anything will ever stimulate him to cast off the community identity and look for a unique life of his own. Although his hot-headed, intelligent, marvellously idiosyncratic father is a zealous anti-Fascist, the

AMARCORD: the 21st of April is the imaginary wedding day of this pudgy adolescent.

boy is already a member of the *Avantguardisti* youth movement. The death of Titta's mother is a particularly deep loss because it means that there is one less person between him and the wasting humanity that surrounds him. Fellini's interest in Titta and his family balances his justifiably snide disdain for most of the other characters. The fact that Titta could be one of any number of youngsters growing up in the area makes the implications of *Amarcord* more serious than if he were an isolated case. The affection Fellini shows is not for all the youth of the town, however, but for the one he has followed through adolescent games, a ribald sexual encounter, the delirium of a fever and a devastating death in the family.

After the conclave with the students in *Roma*, Fellini wondered how he could ever take on the problems of society "when this film director can't even solve his own personal problems." Fellini has always maintained that he cannot confront the public issues until he is on the way toward settling his private internal conflicts. Of course, even the most naive observer would not brand *Amarcord* as political or ideological but Fellini, while pleading the case of the individual, has begun to deal with larger problems.

Filmography

This filmography is divided into two parts. The first lists Fellini's cinema work excluding the films he has directed. In this section I have included the titles and directors of films on which Fellini collaborated. Additional credits are listed when the individual in question has made a contribution to Fellini's cinema career. The second part list Fellini's films as director with whatever credits are available.

Before working as a director, Fellini worked as a gag writer on the following films: *Lo vedi come sei (Do You Know What You Look Like?)* directed by Mario Mattoli, starring Macario, 1939; *No me lo dire (Don't Tell Me)* directed by Mario Mattoli, starring Macario, 1940; *Il pirato sono io (I Am the Pirate)* directed by Mattoli, starring Macario.

Fellini collaborated on the following screenplays: *Documento Z₃ (Document Z₃)* directed by Alfredo Guarini, 1941; *Quarta pagina (The Fourth Page)* directed by Nicola Manzari and Domenico Gambino, 1942; *Avanti, c'é posto (Come On, There's Room)* directed by Mario Bonnard, with Aldo Fabrizi, 1942; *Chi l'ha visto (Who Has Seen Him?)*, directed by Goffredo Alessandrini, 1942; *Campo dei fiori (Field of Flowers)* directed by Mario Bonnard, with Aldo Fabrizi, 1942; *Apparizione* directed by Jean de Limur, 1943; *L'ultima carrozzella (The Last Roundabout)* directed by Mario Mattoli from an idea by Aldo Fabrizi, 1943; *Tutta la città canta (The Whole City Sings)* directed by Riccardo Freda.

Fellini was a scriptwriter and assistant director on *Roma, città aperta (Open City or Rome, Open City)*. Directed by Roberto Rossellini with Aldo Fabrizi, Anna Magnani. Also working on the script were Sergio Amidei, Alberto Consiglio and Rossellini, 1945.

Fellini collaborated on the screenplay for *Il delitto di Giovanni Episcopo (The*

Crime of Giovanni Episcopo/Flesh Will Surrender) directed by Alberto Lattuada from the novel by d'Annunzio, 1946.

Fellini acted as assistant director on *Paisà* directed by Roberto Rossellini. He also worked on the script, contributing especially to the Florence episode and the idea for the Franciscan monastery episode, 1946.

Fellini collaborated on the screenplay of *Senza Pietà (Without Pity)* directed by Alberto Lattuada. Tullio Pinelli also worked on this script. 1947.

Fellini contributed the story, worked on the script and played the part of the phoney St. Joseph in *Il miracolo (The Miracle)*, Roberto Rossellini's segment of *L'amore*. Tullio Pinelli also worked on the screenplay and Anna Magnani starred. 1948.

Fellini collaborated on the screenplay for *In nome della legge (In the Name of the Law/Mafia)* directed by Pietro Germi. Pinelli also collaborated on the script along with Aldo Bizzarri, Giuseppe Mangione, Mario Monicelli and Germi. 1948.

Fellini collaborated on the screen play for *Il mulino del Po (The Mill on the Po)* directed by Alberto Lattuada. Pinelli, Riccardo Bacchelli, Mario Bonfanti, Carlo Musso, Sergio Romono and Lattuada also worked on the script. Carla del Poggio and Jacques Sernas starred. 1948.

Fellini collaborated with Rossellini on the screenplay for *Francesco giullare di*

175

dio (*Flowers of St. Francis*) which Rossellini directed. Otello Martelli did the photography and Aldo Fabrizi starred. 1949.

Fellini collaborated on the screenplay for *Il cammino della speranza* (*The Road to Hope*) directed by Pietro Germi. Germi and Pinelli also worked on the script.

Fellini collabroated on the screenplays of the following films: *La città si difende* (*Passport to Hell/Four Ways Out*) directed by Pietro Germi, 1951; *Il brigante di Tacco del Lupo* directed by Germi, 1952; *Europa '51* directed by Rossellini, 1952; *Fortunella* directed by Eduardo De Filippo. Pinelli and Ennio Flaiano also worked on the script. Giulietta Masina, Alberto Sordi and Paul Douglas starred. 1958.

Fellini has appeared in the following films (in addition to *Il miracolo*): *Ciao Federico* directed by Gideon Bachmann, Produced by Victor Herbert. 1970. 60 minutes. *Ciao Federico* is a documentary consisting of interviews with Fellini and

his co-workers, footage shot on location and in the studio during the making of *Satyricon* and extraneous material that Bachmann has thrown in for no apparent reason. Bachmann's self-indulgence is annoying, but the glimpses of Fellini at work are fascinating. American distributor: Macmillan Audio Brandon.

Alex in Wonderland, directed by Paul Mazursky. Starring Donald Sutherland, Ellen Burstyn, Jeanne Moreau. Produced for M-G-M. This is Mazursky's infantile attempt at his own *8½*. Fellini appears briefly in a *hommage* that seems more like hero worship. American distributors: United Artists (35 mm), Films, Inc. (16mm).

FILMS DIRECTED BY FELLINI
(Titles in italics are English-language release titles, and not necessarily translations)
1950: LUCI DEL VARIETA (*Lights of Variety/Variety Lights*) (Italy). Produced by Fellini and Alberto Lattuada

VARIETY LIGHTS: Parmasani's show.

THE WHITE SHEIK: Brunella Bova's Wanda swoons over her hero, the White Sheik.

for Capitolium, Rome. *Dir:* Fellini and Alberto Lattuada. *Scr:* Fellini, Ennio Flaiano, Alberto Lattuada, Tullio Pinelli, from a story by Fellini. *Ph:* Otello Martelli. *Art dir:* Aldo Buzzi. *Music:* Felice Lattuada. *Edit:* Mario Bonotti. 93 mins. [U.S. distribution: Contemporary Films (35mm), Macmillan Audio Brandon (16mm); U.K.: Gala (35mm), BFI (16mm)]

CAST: Peppino De Filippo (*Checco Dalmonte*), Giulietta Masina (*Melina Amour*), Carla Del Poggio (*Liliana*), Folco Lulli (*Conti, the Lover*), John Kitzmiller (*Johnny, the Trumpet Player*), Dante Maggio (*Remo, the Comedian*), Carlo Romano (*Renzo, the Lawyer*), Giulio Cali (*Edison Will, the Swami*), Franca Valeri (*Designer*), Silvio Bagolini (*Journalist*), Gina Mascetti, Caprioli and Bonucci, Nando Bruno.

1952: LO SCEICCO BIANCO (*The White Sheik*) (Italy). Produced by Luigi Rovere for PDC. *Dir:* Fellini. *Scr:* Fellini, Ennio Flaiano, Tullio Pinelli, from a story by Fellini, Tullio Pinelli

and Michelangelo Antonioni. *Ph:* Arturo Gallea. *Cam. op:* Antonio Belviso. *Architect:* Raffaelo Tolfo. *Sound:* Armando Grilli, Walfredo Traversari. *Music:* Nino Rota. *Music dir:* Fernando Previtale. *Edit:* Rolando Benedetti. *Make-Up:* Franco. 86 mins. [U.S.: Contemporary Films (35mm), Macmillan Audio Brandon 16mm)]

CAST: Alberto Sordi (*Fernando Rivoli, "The White Sheik"*), Leopoldo Trieste (*Ivan Cavalli*), Brunella Bovo (*Wanda Cavalli*), Giulietta Masina (*Cabiria*), Ernesto Almirante (*Director of "White Sheik" strip*), Fanny Marchiò (*Marilena Velardi, Woman in fumetti Office*), Ettore M. Margadonna (*Ivan's Uncle*), Jole Silvani, Anna Primula, Lilia Landi, Gina Mascetti, Enzo Maggio, Nino Billi, Armando Libianchi, Ugo Attanasio, Elettra Zago, Giulio Moreschi, Piero Antonucci, Aroldino.

1953: I VITELLONI/LES VITELLONI (*The Spivs/The Young and the Passionate*) (Italy/France). Produced by Lorenzo Pegoraro for PEG Films/Cité Films. *Dir:* Fellini, *Ass. dir:* Max de

lucorbeil, Moraldo Rossi. *Scr*: Fellini, Ennio Flaiano, from a story by Fellini, Ennio Flaiano, and Tullio Pinelli. *Ph*: Otello Martelli, Luciano Trasatti, Carlo Carlini. *Cam. op*: Roberto Girardi, Franco Villa. *Art dir*: Mario Chiari. *Music*: Nino Rota. *Cond*: Franco Ferrara. *Edit*: Rolando Benedetti. *Cost*: M. Marinari, Bomarzi. 104 mins. [U.S.: Contemporary Films (35mm), Contemporary Films (16mm); U.K.: Connoisseur Films (16mm)]
CAST: Franco Interlenghi (*Moraldo*), Albert Sordi (*Alberto*), Franco Fabrizi (*Fausto*), Leopoldo Trieste (*Leopoldo*), Riccardo Fellini (*Riccardo*), Eleonora Ruffo (*Sandra*), Jean Brochard (*Fausto's Father*), Carlo Romano (*Michele, Fausto's Employer*), Lida Baarowa (*Giulia, Michele's Wife*), Claude Farère (*Alberto's Sister*), Enrico Viarisio (*Sandra's Father*), Paola Borboni (*Sandra's Mother*), Maja Nipora (*Chanteuse*), Vira Silenti (*Cinesina, Leopoldo's date*), Arlette Sauvage (*Dark Lady in Theatre*), Achille Majeroni, Guido Marturi, Silvio Bagolini, Milvia Chianelli, Gondrano Trucchi, Franca Gandolfi, Giovanna Galli.

1953: AMORE IN CITTA (*Love in the City*). (Italy). Episode: *Un agenzia matrimoniale* (*A Matrimonial Agency*). Produced by Cesare Zavattini, Renato Ghione, Marco Ferrere for Faro Films. *Dir*: Fellini. *Scr*: Fellini and Tullio Pinelli. *Ph*: Gianni Di Venanzo. *Art dir*: Gianni Polidori. *Music*: Mario Nascimbene. *Edit*: Eraldo Da Roma. c. 20 mins. [U.S.: Macmillan Audio Brandon]
CAST: Antonio Cifariello, non-professional actors from the Centro Sperimentale di Cinematografia, and non-actors recreating their own stories. Other episodes by Dino Risi, Michelangelo Antonioni, Alberto Lattuada, Francesco Maselli, Carlo Lizzani, Cesare Zavattini, and Luciano Emmer.

1954: LA STRADA (Italy). Produced by Carlo Ponti and Dino De Laurentiis. *Dir*: Fellini. *Scr*: Fellini, Ennio Flaiano, Tullio Pinelli, from a story by Fellini and Tullio Pinelli. *Ph*: Otello Martelli. *Art dir*: Mario Ravasco. *Music*: Nino Rota. *Cond*: Franco Ferrara. *Edit*: Leo Cattozzo. 107 mins. [U.S.: Janus Films; U.K.: Contemporary Films]
CAST: Giulietta Masina (*Gelsomina*), Anthony Quinn (*Zampano*), Richard Basehart (*Il Matto*), Aldo Silvani (*Colombaioni, the Circus Owner*), Marcella Rovena (*La Vedora*), Lidia Venturini.

LA STRADA: Gelsomina's isolation is visually apparent when she throws herself into a ditch.

NIGHTS OF CABIRIA: Oscar betrays Cabiria.

1955: IL BIDONE: (*The Swindlers/ The Swindle*) (Italy/France). Produced for Titanus/SGC. *Dir*: Fellini. *Scr*: Fellini, Ennio Flaiano, Tullio Pinelli. *Ph*: Otello Martelli. *Cam. op*: Roberto Gerardi. *Art dir*: Dario Cecchi. *Sound*: Giovanni Rossi. *Music*: Nino Rota. *Cond*: Franco Ferrara. *Edit*: Mario Serandrei, Giuseppe Vari. *Cost*: Dario Cecchi. *Set dec*: Massimiliano Capriccioli. *Make-Up*: Eligio Trani. *Artistic collab*: Brunello Rondi. 92 mins. [U.S.: Macmillan Audio Brandon; U.K.: Connoisseur Films]
CAST: Broderick Crawford (*Augusto*), Giulietta Masina (*Iris*), Richard Basehart (*Picasso*), Franco Fabrizi (*Roberto*), Lorella De Luca (*Patrizia*), Giacomo Gabrielli (*Vargas*), Alberto De Amicis (*Goffredo*), Irene Cefaro (*Marisa, the Girl at Rinaldo's Party*), Sue Ellen Blake (*Anna*), Xenia Valderi, Maria Zanoli, Mario Passante, Lucietta Muratori, Riccardo Garrone, Paul Grenter.
1956: LE NOTTI DI CABIRIA (*Nights of Cabiria*) (Italy). Produced by Dino De Laurentiis. *Dir*: Fellini. *Ass. dirs*: Moraldo Rossi, Dominique Delouche. *Scr*: Fellini, Ennio Flaiano, Tullio

Pinelli. *Addit. dial*: Pier Paolo Pasolini. *Ph*: Aldo Tonti and Otello Martelli. *Art dir*: Piero Gherardi. *Music*: Nino Rota. *Cond*: Franco Ferrara. *Edit*: Leo Cattozzo. 110 mins. [U.S.: Macmillan Audio Brandon; U.K.: Connoisseur (16mm)]
CAST: Giulietta Masina (*Cabiria*), François Périer (*Oscar*), Amedeo Nazzari (*Mario, The Actor*), Aldo Silvani (*Hypnotist*), Franca Marzi (*Wanda*), Dorian Gray (*Jessy*), Mario Passante (*Cripple*), Pina Gualandri (*Matilda, Cabiria's Enemy*), Franco Fabrizi (*Giorgio*), Ennio Girolami, Christian Tassou.
1960: LA DOLCE VITA/ LA DOUCEUR DE VIVRE (*The Sweet Life*) (Italy/France). Produced by Giuseppe Amato and Angelo Rizzoli for Riama Film, Rome/Pathé Consortium Cinema-Gray Film, Paris. *Dir*: Fellini. *Ass. dirs*: Giancarlo Romani, Gianfranco Mingozzi, Lilli Veenman. *Scr*: Fellini, Ennio Flaiano, Tullio Pinelli, Brunello Rondi. *Ph*: Otello Martelli (Totalscope). *Cam. op*: Arturo Zavattini. *Art dir*: Piero Gherardi (assisted by Giorgio Giovannini and Lucia Mirisola, Vito Anzalone), *Sound*: Agostino Moretti. *Music*: Nino

LA DOLCE VITA: Marcello and fellow revellers return briefly to the sea.

Rota. *Cond*: Franco Ferrara, with I. Campanino and Adriano Celentano. *Edit*: Leo Cattozzo. *Make-Up*: Otello Fava. *Artistic collab*: Brunello Rondi. 173 mins. [U.S.: American International Pictures (35mm), Macmillan Audio Brandon (16mm); U.K.: Eagle Films (35mm), Darvill Associates (16mm).] CAST: Marcello Mastroianni (*Marcello Rubini*), Anouk Aimée (*Maddalena*), Yvonne Furneaux (*Emma*), Anita Ekberg (*Sylvia*), Alain Cuny (*Steiner*), Annibale Ninchi (*Marcello's Father*), Valeria Ciangottini (*Paola*), Lex Barker (*Robert, Sylvia's Fiancé*), Giulio Paradisi (*First Photographer*), Enzo Cerusico (*Second Photographer*), Adriana Moneta (*Prostitute*), Harriet White (*Edna, Sylvia's Secretary*), Carlo Di Maggio (*Toto Scalise, Sylvia's Producer*), Alain Dijon (*Frankie Stout*), Giacomo Gabriello (*Maddalena's Father*), Alfredo Rizzi (*Television Director*), Rina Franchetti (*Mother of the Miracle Children*), Aurelio Nardi (*Uncle of the Miracle Children*), Giovanna and Massimo (*Miracle Children*), Renée Longarini (*Mrs. Steiner*), Vittorio Manfrino (*Maître d' at the Kit Kat*), Polidor (*Clown with Balloons*), Magali Noël (*Fanny, Chorus Girl at the Kit Kat*), Enzo Doria (*Third Photographer*), Lilli Granado (*Lucy*), Gloria Jones (*Gloria*), Nello Meniconi (*Angry Man on Via Veneto*), Massimo Busetti (*Pierrone*), Nico Otzak (*Nico*), Audrey McDonald (*Sonia*), Prince Vadim Wolkonsky (*Owner of Castle*), Ferdinando Brofferio (*Maddalena's Lover at Castle*), Ida Galli (*Debutante*), Giulio Girola (*Policeman*), Nadia Gray (*Nadia*), Mino Doro (*Nadia's Lover*), Carlo Musto (*Carlo*), Antonio Jacono (*Domino*), Sandra Lee (*Spoleto Dancer*), Jacques Sernas (*Matinee Idol*), Leontine van Strein (*Matinee Idol's Mistress*), Leo Coleman (*Black Dancer*), Laura Betti (*Laura*), Tito Buzzo (*Muscleman*), Henry Thody, John Francis Lane, Donatella Della Nora, Donato Castellaneta (*Journalists at Sylvia's Press Conference*), Iris Tree (*Iris, Guest at Steiner's Party*), Giulio Questi (*Don Giulio*), Doris Pignatelli (*Aristocrat*), Eugenio Ruspoli (*Aristocrat*), Leonida Repaci (*Writer at Steiner's*), Walter

Santesso (*Paparazzo*), Daniela Calvino, Franca Pasutt, Enrico Glori.

1962: BOCCACCIO '70 (Italy/France). Episode: *Le tentazioni del Dottor Antonio* (*The Temptations of Doctor Antonio*). Produced by Carlo Ponti and Antonio Cervi for Concordia Compagnia Cinematografica-Cineriz, Rome/Francinex-Gray Films (Paris). *Dir*: Fellini. *Scr*: Fellini, Ennio Flaiano, Tullio Pinelli. *Collab*: Brunello Rondi and Goffredo Parise. *Ph*: Otello Martelli (Eastmancolor). *Art dir*: Piero Zuffi. *Music*: Nino Rota. *Edit*: Leo Cattozzo. [U.S.: Avco Embassy Pictures; U.K.: Avco Embassy (35mm)]

CAST: Peppino DeFilippo (*Dr. Antonio Mazzuolo*), Anita Ekberg (*Anita*), Antonio Acqua (*Commendator La Pappa*), Donatella Della Nora (*Antonio's Sister*), Eleanora Maggi (*Cupid*).Monique Berger, Giacomo Furia, Alberto Sorrentino, Mario Passante, Silvio Bagolino.

Other episodes by Vittorio De Sica, Luchino Visconti and Mario Monicelli. The film was co-ordinated by Cesare Zavattini.

1963: OTTO E MEZZO (*8½*) (Italy).

Produced by Angelo Rizzoli. *Dir*: Fellini. *Scr*: Fellini, Ennio Flaiano, Tullio Pinelli, Brunello Rondi, from a story by Fellini and Ennio Flaiano. *Ph*: Gianni Di Venanzo. *Cam. op*: Pasquale De Santis. *Art dir*: Piero Gherardi. *Sound*: Mario Faraoni and Alberto Bartolomei. *Music*: Nino Rota: *Edit*: Leo Cattozzo. *Ass. edit*: Adriana Olasio. *Cost*: Piero Gherardi. *Set dec*: Vito Anzalo. *Make-Up*: Otello Fava. 135 mins. [U.S.: Avco Embassy Pictures (35mm), Macmillan (35mm), VPS (16mm), BFI (16mm extract)]

CAST: Marcello Mastroianni (*Guido Anselmi*), Anouk Aimée (*Luisa*), Sandra Milo (*Carla*), Claudia Cardinale (*Claudia*), Rossella Falk (*Rossella*), Mario Pisù (*Mozzabotta*), Barbara Steele (*Gloria Morin*), Guido Alberti (*Pace, the Producer*), Jean Rougeul (*Daumier, the Critic*), Madeleine Lebeau (*French Actress*), Caterina Boratto (*Apparation Woman*), Annibale Ninchi (*Guido's Father*), Giuditta Rissone (*Guido's Mother*), Yvonne Casadei (*Jacqueline Bonbon, the Aging Chanteuse*),

8½: a disgruntled Guido—swathed in sheets—listens to complaints about Jacqueline's status in the harem.

Alberto Conochia (*Production Manager*), Ian Dallas (*Master of Ceremonies*), Mary Indovino (*Maya*), Edra Gale (*La Saraghina*), Tito Masini (*Cardinal*), Bruno Agostini (*Production Secretary*), Eugene Walters (*American Journalist*), Gilda Dahlberg (*Journalist's Wife and Magazine Writer*), Annie Gorassini (*Pace's Girl-friend*), Cesarino Miceli Picardi (*Production Inspector*), Mark Herron (*Enrico, Luisa's satellite*), Mario Conocchia (*Director*), John Stacy (*Accountant*), Elisabetta Catalano (*Luisa's Sister*), Alfredo De Lafeld (*Cardinal's Secretary*), Frazier Rippy (*Advance Man for the Cardinal*), Maria Tedeschi (*Father Superior*), Georgia Simmons (*Guido's Grandmother*), Nadine Sanders (*Stewardess*), Hedy Vessel (*Girl in Harem Sequence*), Roberto Nicolosi (*Doctor*), Neil Robinson (*French Actress's Agent*), Marco Gemini (*Guido as a Boy*), Riccardo Guglielmi (*Guido as a Boy*), Olimpia Cavalli (*Actress Playing Carla in Screen Test*), Sonia Gensner (*Actress Playing Luisa in Screen Test*), Hazel Scott (*Black Woman in Harem*), Rosella Como, Francesco Rigamonti, Matilde Calnam (*Luisa's friends*).

1965: GIULIETTA DEGLI SPIRITI (*Juliet of the Spirits*) (Italy). Produced by Angelo Rizzoli for Federiz. *Dir*: Fellini. *Scr*: Fellini, Tullio Pinelli, Brunello Rondi, Ennio Flaiano, from a story by Fellini and Tullio Pinelli. *Ph*: Gianni Di Venanzo (Technicolor). *Art dir*: Piero Gherardi. *Music*: Nino Rota. *Cond*: Carlo Savina. *Edit*: Ruggero Mastroianni. *Cost*: Piero Gherardi. *Set dec*: Luciano Riccieri, E. Benazzi Taglietti, Giantito Burchiellaro. *Make-Up*: Otello Fava, Eligio Trani. 145 mins. [U.S.: Cinemation Industries (35mm), Macmillan Audio Brandon (16mm); U.K.: Connoisseur]
CAST: Giulietta Masina (*Giulietta*), Mario Pisù (*Giorgio*), Sandra Milo (*Susy/Fanny/Iris*), Caterina Boratto (*Giulietta's Mother*), Luisa Della Noce (*Adele, Giulietta's Sister*), Sylva Koscina (*Sylva, Giulietta's Sister*), Lou Gilbert (*Giulietta's Grandfather*), Valentina Cortese (*Val*), Silvano Jachino, (*Dolores*), Elena Fondra (*Elena*), José de Villalonga (*José*), Valeska Gert (*Bhishma*), Asoka Rubener (*Bhishma's Male Assistant*), Sujata Rubener (*Female Assistant*), Walter Harrison (*Assistant*), Edoardo Torricella (*Russian Teacher*),

Alberto Plebani (*Lynx-Eyes*), Felice Fulchignoni (*Giulietta's Doctor*), Anne Francine (*Psychoanalyst*), Mario Conochia (*Lawyer*), Genius (*Medium*), Alba Cancelliere (*Giulietta as a Child*), Fredrich Ledebur (*Headmaster*), Cesarino Miceli Picardi (*Giorgio's Friend*), Federico Valli (*Valli*), Remo Risaliti, Grillo Rufino (*Lynx-Eyes's Employees*), Dany Paris (*Desperate Friend*), Irina Alexeieva (*Susy's Grandmother*), Massimo Sarchielli (*Val's Lover*), Fred Williams (*Indian Lover*), Raffaele Guida (*Oriental Lover*), Alessandra Mannoukine (*Susy's Mother*), Gilberto Galvan (*Susy's Chauffeur*), Seyna Seyn (*Susy's Masseuse*), Hildgarde Golez, Yvonne Casadei, Dina De Santis (*Susy's Maids*), Sabrina Gigli, Rossella Di Sepio (*Little Grand-daughters*), Alba Rosa (*Dolores's Female Model*), Nadir Moretti (*Male Model*), Milena Vukotic, Elisabetta Pitio Gray (*Giulietta's Maids*), Giorgio Ardisson, Bob Edwards.

1968: HISTOIRES EXTRAORDINAIRES/TRE PASSI NEL DELIRIO (*Tales of Mystery/Spirits of the Dead*) (France/Italy). Episode: *Il ne faut jamais parier sa tête avec le diable/Toby Dammit*. Produced by Raymond Eger for Les Films Marceau-Cocinor, Paris/PEA, Rome. *Dir*: Fellini. *Ass. dir*: Eschilo Tarquini. *Scr*: Fellini, Bernardino Zapponi, liberally adapted from "Never Bet the Devil Your Head" by Edgar Allan Poe. *Ph*: Giuseppe Rotunno (Eastmancolor, scope). *Cam. op*: Giuseppe Maccari. *Art dir*: Fabrizio Clerici. *Music*: Nino Rota. *Edit*: Ruggero Mastroianni. *Ass. edit*: Adriana Olasio. *Cost. and set dec*: Piero Tosi. *Spec. effects*: Joseph Natanson. c. 40 mins. [U.S.: American International Pictures (35mm), United Films (16mm); U.K.: Cinecenta (35mm)]
CAST: Terence Stamp (*Toby Dammit*), Salvo Randone (*Priest*), Antonia Pietrosi (*Actress*), Polidor (*Old Actor*), Fabrizio Angeli, Ernesto Colli, Marina Yaru, Aleardo Ward, Paul Cooper.

1968: FELLINI: A DIRECTOR'S NOTEBOOK (U.S.A.). Produced for NBC-TV. *Dir*: Fellini. *Scr*: Fellini. *Ph*: Pasquale De Santis (colour). 54 mins. [U.S.: Twyman Films (16mm); U.K.: BFI (16mm)]
CAST: Fellini, Giulietta Masina, Mar-

TOBY DAMMIT: when the gridwork of lights is switched on, it is necessary to readjust our perception of the shot.

cello Mastroianni, Genius the Medium, Pasquale De Santis, Marina Boratto.
1969: SATYRICON/FELLINI-SATYRICON (*Fellini-Satyricon*) (Italy/France). Produced by Alberto Grimaldi for PEA, Rome/Les Productions Artistes Associés, Paris. *Dir*: Fellini. *Ass. dir*: Maurizio Mein. *Scr*: Fellini and Bernardino Zapponi, freely adapted from the work by Petronius Arbiter. *Ph*: Giuseppe Rotunno (Technicolor). *Cam. op*: Giuseppe Macari. *Art dir*: Danilo Donati (scenery sketches by Fellini). *Music*: Nino Rota, Ilhan Mimaroglu, Tod Dockstader, Andrew Rudin. *Edit*: Ruggero Mastroianni. *Ass. edit*: Adriana Olasio. *Cost*: Danilo Donati. *Make-Up*: Rino Carboni. *Spec. effects*: Adriano Pischiutta. *Latin language cons*: Luca Canali. 127 mins. [U.S.: United Artists; U.K.: United Artists (35mm), FDA (16mm)]
CAST: Martin Potter (*Encolpio*), Hiram Keller (*Ascylto*), Max Born (*Giton*), Fanfulla (*Vernacchio*), Salvo Randone (*Eumolpo*),Mario Romagnoli "Il More" (*Trimalchio*), Magali Noël (*Fortunata*), Giuseppe San Vitale (*Habinnas*), Alain Cuny (*Lichas*), Capucine (*Tryphaena*), Lucia Bosé (*Matron*), Joseph Wheeler (*Suicide*), Hylette Adolphe (*Slave Girl*), Tanya Lopert (*Emperor*), Luigi Montefiori (*Minotaur*), Marcello Difolco (*Proconsul*), Elisa Mainardi (*Ariadne*), Donyale Luna (*Oenothea*), Carlo Giordana (*Captain*), Gordon Mitchell (*Thief*), Genius-Eugenio Mastropietro (*Parvenu, the Freedman*), Pasquale Baldassare (*Hermaphrodite*), Danica La Loggia (*Scintilla*), Antonia Pietrosi (*Widow of Ephesus*), Wolfgang Hillinger (*Soldier at Ephesus Tomb*), Elio Gigante (*Owner of Garden of Delights*), Sibilla Sedat (*Nymphomaniac*), Lorenzo Piani (*Nymphomaniac's Husband*), Luigi Zerbinati (*Nymphomaniac's Slave*), Vittorio Vittori (*Notary*), Suleiman Ali Nashnush (*Tryphaena's Attendant*), Luigi Battaglia (*Transvestite*), Tania Duckworth (*Brothel Girl*), Maria De Sisti (*Fat Woman*).
1970: I CLOWNS/LES CLOWNS (*The Clowns*) (Italy/France/W. Germany) Produced by Elio Scardamaglia and Ugo Guerra for RAI-TV and Compagnia Leone Cinematografica, Rome/ORTF, Paris/Bavaria Film, W. Germany. *Dir*: Fellini. *Ass. dir*: Maurizio Mein. *Scr*: Fellini and Bernardino Zapponi. *Ph*: Dario Di Palma (Technicolor). *Cam. op*: Blasco Giurato. *Art dir*: Danilo Donati. *Sound*: Alberto Bartolomei. *Music*: Nino Rota. *Cond*: Carlo Savina.

Edit: Ruggero Mastroianni. *Ass. edit*: Adriana Olasio. *Cost*: Danilo Donati. *Set dec*: Renzo Gronchi. *Make-Up*: Rino Carboni. 90 mins. [U.S.: Levitt-Pickman Film (35mm), Films Inc. (16mm); U.K.: Curzon Film Distributors (35mm)] CAST: THE CLOWNS: Riccardo Billi, Tino Scotti, Fanfulla, Carlo Rizzo, Freddo Pistoni, Furia, Reder, Valentini, 14 Colombaioni, Merli, I Martana, Maggio, Sbarra, Carini, Terzo, Vingelli, Fumagalli, Zerbinati, Janigro, Maunsell, Peverello, Sorrentino, Valdemaro Bevilacqua. FELLINI'S TROUPE: Fellini, Maya Morin, Lina Alberti, Alvaro Vitale, Gasparino. THE FRENCH CLOWNS: Alex, Bario, Père Loriot, Ludo, Mais, Nino. THEMSELVES: Liana Orfei, Rinaldo Orfei, Nando Orfei, Pierre Etaix, Gustav Fratellini, Tristan Rémy, Annie Fratellini, Baptiste, Anita Ekberg, Franco Migliorini the Lion-Tamer, Victoria Chaplin.

1972: ROMA (*Fellini-Roma/Fellini's Roma*) (Italy/France). Produced by Turi Vasile for Ultra Film, Rome/Les Artistes Associés, Paris. *Dir*: Fellini. *Ass. dir*: Maurizio Mein. *Scr*: Fellini and Bernardino Zapponi. *Ph*: Giuseppe Rotunno (Technicolor). *Cam. op*: Giuseppe Maccari. *Art dir*: Danilo Donati. *Music*: Nino Rota. *Cond*: Carlo Savina. *Edit*: Ruggero Mastroianni. *Ass. edit*: Adriana Olasio. *Cost*: Danilo Donati. *Make-Up*: Rino Carboni. *Spec. effects*: Adriano Pischiutta. *Choreo*: Gino Landi. 128 mins. (outside Italy). [U.S.: United Artists; U.K.: United Artists (35mm), FDA (16mm)] CAST: Peter Gonzales (*Young Fellini*), Fiona Florence (*Charming Prostitute*), Pia De Doses (*Princess of Black Aristocracy*), Libero Frissi (*Opening Dancer in "Bolero" Act at Music Hall*), Mario Del Vago, Galliano Sbarra, Alfredo Adami, Bireno, Valdemaro (*Performers in Music-Hall*), Alvaro Vitale, (*Tap Dancer Imitating Fred Astaire in Music-Hall*), Britta Barnes, Marne Maitland, Renato Giovannoli, Elisa Mainardi, Paule Rout, Paola Natale, Marcelle Ginette Bron, Stefano Mayore, and Anna Magnani, Gore Vidal, Alberto Sordi and Marcello Mastroianno (*Themselves*). (Note: Sordi and Mastroianni were cut from the version distributed outside Italy.)

1974: AMARCORD (Italy/France). Produced by Franco Cristaldi for FC Productions, Rome/PECF, Paris. *Dir*: Fellini. *Ass. dir*: Maurizio Mein. *Scr*: Fellini and Tonino Guerra. *Ph*: Giuseppe Rotunno. *Cam. op*: Giuseppe Maccari. *Art dir*: Danilo Donati. *Sound*: Oscar De Arcangelis. *Music*: Nino Rota. *Cond*: Carlo Savina. *Edit*: Ruggero Mastroianni. *Ass. edit*: Adriana Olasio. *Cost*: Danilo Donati. *Make-Up*: Rino Carboni. *Spec. effects*: Adriano Pischiutta. 123 mins. [U.S.: New World Pictures; Films, Inc. (16mm) ; U.K.: Columbia-Warner.] CAST: Pupella Maggio (*Titta's Mother*), Armando Brancia (*Aurelio, Titta's Father*), Bruno Zanin (*Titta*), Stefano Proietti (*Oliva*), Peppino Ianigro (*Titta's Grandfather*), Nandino Orfei (*Il Pataca*), Carla Mora (*La Cameriera*), Ciccio Ingrassia (*Mad Uncle*), Magali Noël ("*Gradisca*"), Luigi Rossi (*Lawyer*), Maria Antonella Belizzi (*Tobacconist*), Josiane Tanzilli (*Volpina*), Gennaro Ombra (*Biscein, the Liar*), Gianfilippo Carcano (*Don Balosa*), Aristide Caporale (*Giudizio*), Ferruccio Brembilla (*Il Gerarca del Borgo*), Antonino Faà di Bruno (*Conte di Lovignano*), Gianfranco Marrocco (*Conte Poltavo*), Alvaro Vitale (*Naso*), Bruno Scagnetti (*Ovo*), Bruno Lenzi (*Gigliozzi*), Fernando de Felice (*Ciccio*), Francesco Vona (*Candela*), Donatella Gambini (*Aldina Cordini*), Franco Magno (*Zeus*), Mauro Misul (*Philosophy Teacher*), Armando Villella (*Greek Teacher*), Dina Adorni (*Maths Teacher*), Francesco Maselli (*Science Teacher*), Mario Silvestri (*Italian Teacher*), Fides Stagni (*Fine Arts Teacher*), Marcello Bonini Olas (*Gym Teacher*), Domenico Pertica (*Blindman of Cantarel*), Fausto Signoretti (*Madonna, the Coach Driver*), Fredo Pistoni (*Colonia*), Mario Nebolini (*Segretario Comunale*), Vincenzo Caldarola (*Mendicante*), Mario Liberati ("*Ronald Coleman," Proprietor of the Fulgor*), Fiorella Magalotti (*Gradisca's Sister*), Marina Trovalusci (*Gradisca's Little Sister*), Milo Mario (*Photographer*), Antonio Spaccatini (*Federale*), Bruno Bartocci (*Gradisca's Husband*), Marco Laurentino (*Mutilated War Veteran*), Riccardo Satta (*Sensale*), Carmela Eusepi (*Contessina Lovignano*), Clemente Baccherini (*Proprietor of the Cafe Commercio*), Marcello di Falco (*Il Principe*), Constantino Serraino (*Gigino Penna Bianca*).

1975: CASANOVA (in production at time of writing) .

Bibliography

A. *Books and monographs on Fellini*

1. Agel, Geneviève. "Les chemins de Fellini." Paris, Editions du Cerf, 1956.
2. American Film Institute "Federico Fellini" (edited by James Silke). Washington, AFI Center for Advanced Film Studies, 1970
3. Boyer, Deena. "The Two Hundred Days of 8½," translated by Charles Lam Markmann with an afterword by Dwight Macdonald. New York, The Macmillan Co., 1964.
4. Budgen, Suzanne. "Fellini." London, British Film Institute, 1966.
5. Buono, Oreste Del. "Federico Fellini." Monza, Circolo Monzese del Cinema. (Cinestudio no. 14)
6. Goldberg, Toby. "Federico Fellini: a Poet of Reality." Boston University, Broadcasting and Film Division, 1965.
7. Joseph, Rudolph S., (editor). "Der Regisseur Federico Fellini." Munich, Photo und Filmmuseum, Münchner Stadtmuseum, 1970.
8. Radiodiffusion-Television Belge. "Entretiens avec Federico Fellini: Textes extrait des émissions télévisées "La double vue." Brussels, Radiodiffusion-Television Belge, 1962.
9. Rondi, Brunello. "Il cinema di Fellini." Rome, Bianco & Nero, 1965. (Personalita della storia del cinema no. 3)
10. Ross, Lillian. "10½ a movie in technicolor." From "New Yorker," October 30th, 1965.
11. Salachas, Gilbert. "Federico Fellini." Paris, Seghers, 1963.
   —English edition: New York, Crown Publishers, 1969.
12. Solmi, Angelo. "Fellini" (Translated by Elizabeth Greenwood). New York, Merlin Press, 1967.

B. *Books with Sections on Fellini*

13. Baldelli, Pio. "Dilatazione visionaria del documento e nostalgia della madre chiesa in Fellini," in "Cinema dell'ambiguita. Vol 1." Rome, Samona e Savelli, 1971.

14. Bory, Jean-Louis. "Pour et Contre Fellini," in "Les Yeux pour Voir: Cinema I." Paris, Union Generale d'Editions, 1971.

15. Cooper, John C., and Skrade, Carl, editors. "The Purpose of the Grotesque in Fellini's Films," by Harvey G. Cox, in "Celluloid and Symbols." Philadelphia, Fortress Press, 1970.

16. Cowie, Peter. "Federico Fellini," in "50 Major Film-Makers." London, Tantivy Press; New York, A.S. Barnes, 1975.

17. Fallaci, Oriana. "Federico Fellini: Famous Italian Director," in "Limelighters." Michael Joseph, 1967.

18. Fellini, Federico. "My Experiences as a Director," in "International Film Annual No. 3." John Calder, 1959.

19. Gregor, Ulrich. "Federico Fellini," in "Wie Sie Filmen." Gütersloh, Sigbert Mohn Verlag, 1966.

20. Harcourt, Peter. "The Secret Life of Federico Fellini," in "Six European Directors." Harmondsworth, Middlesex, Penguin Books, 1974.

21. Rhode, Eric. "Federico Fellini," in "Tower of Babel." Weidenfeld & Nicolson, 1966.

22. Robinson, W.R., editor. "Fellini: Analyst without Portfolio," by Armando Favazza, in "Man and the Movies," Baton Rouge, LSU Press, 1967.

23. Sarris, Andrew, editor. "Federico Fellini" in "Interviews with Film Directors." New York, Bobbs-Merrill, 1967.

24. Taylor, John Russell. "Federico Fellini" in "Cinema Eye, Cinema Ear." London, Methuen; New York, Hill and Wang, 1964.

C. *Published Scripts in English*

25. Fellini, Federico. "Early Screenplay: *Variety Lights, The White Sheik*" New York, Orion Press, 1971.

26. Fellini, Federico. "Three Screenplays: *I vitelloni, Il bidone, The Temptations of Dr. Antonio.*" New York, Orion Press, 1970.

27. Fellini, Federico, "*La dolce vita.*" New York, Ballantine Books, 1961.

28. Fellini, Federico, "*Juliet of the Spirits*, with interview with Fellini" and introduction by Tullio Kezich. New York, Ballantine Books, 1965.

29. Fellini, Federico. "*Satyricon*" edited by Dario Zanelli. New York, Ballantine Books, 1970.

D. *Published Scripts in Italian*

30. Fellini, Federico. "*Le notti di Cabiria,*" edited by Lino Del Fra. Bologna, Cappelli, 1965.

31. Fellini, Federico. "*La dolce vita,*" edited by Tullio Kezich. Rocco San Casciano, Cappelli, 1960.

32. Fellini, Federico. "*8½,*" edited by Camilla Caderna. Bologna, Cappelli, 1963.

33. Fellini, Federico. "*Giulietta degli spiriti,*" edited by Tullio Kezich. Bologna, Cappelli, 1965.

34. Fellini, F., Vadim, R., Malle, L., *"Tre passi nel delirio."* Bologna, Cappelli.
35. Fellini, Federico, *"Fellini Satyricon."* Bologna, Cappelli, 1969.
36. Fellini, Federico and Zapponi: Bernardino, *"Roma,"* Bologna, Cappelli, 1972.
37. Fellini, Federico. "Fellini TV: *Block-notes di un registra; I Clowns."* Bologna, Cappelli, 1972.
38. Fellini, Federico. "Il Film *Amarcord."* Bologna, Cappelli, 1974.
39. Fellini, Federico. "Il primo Fellini: *Lo sceicco bianco; I vitelloni; La strada; Il bidone."* Bologna, Cappelli, 1974.

E. *By Fellini*

40. Fellini, Federico (with Tonino Guerra). "Amarcord, Portrait of a Town" London, Abelard-Schuman, 1974.
41. Fellini, Federico. "Fellini Vogue," in French "Vogue," December 1972-January, 1974.

F. *General*

42. Armes, Roy. "Patterns of Realism," Cranbury, New Jersey, A.S. Barnes and Co./London, The Tantivy Press, 1971.
43. Bazin, André. "What is Cinema?" Berkeley and Los Angeles, University of California Press, 1971.
44. Geduld, Harry, editor. "Filmmakers on Filmmaking." Bloomington, Indiana, Indiana University Press, 1969.

Fellini: shooting AMARCORD.

Index

DATE			